KINTBURY

A Century Remembered

1900 - 1999

Published by the Kintbury Volunteer Group

As sponsors, the Kintbury Volunteer Group much appreciate the contribution made by Sybil Flinn in editing, cajoling, researching, enlisting the skills of others, and using her own experience to bring about the publication of this book.

Thank you, Sybil!

Kintbury Volunteer Group
Thatcher's Yard
Church Street
Kintbury, Berks. RG17 9TR.

ISBN 0 947612 35 1

Book designed and produced by Mike English.
Typeset and prepared for production by
M&C Saatchi Ltd.

Printed in Great Britain by
WBC Book Manufacturers Ltd., Bridgend.

Contents

Introduction

The inspiration for this book was *1,000 Years of Kintbury* by Thora Morrish and Margaret Yates, and also the various talks given by Thora and Margaret over the past ten years. However, I believe intentionally, the authors stopped their narrative at the beginning of the twentieth century. This seemed a pity and I felt that with the Millennium fast approaching it would be appropriate to bring the Kintbury story up to date, as the changes in the past century have been tremendous and there were many memories of these changes to be recorded.

The Kintbury Volunteer Group decided to adopt the production of this book as its Millennium project and I set to work approaching people who might be able to write on particular subjects, and others who had memories to relate. Part way through, it became clear that if the book was to be completed on time, extra help was needed. At this stage, Heather Turner, Chairman of the Kintbury Volunteer Group, who had from the outset been an enthusiastic supporter of the project, stepped in with practical help and it is largely due to her efforts that the book has been produced. Thank you, Heather, for all the research and authorship you have contributed to this work. I must also give thanks to Mike English, who designed and produced the book and, in particular, to M&C Saatchi Ltd., for typesetting and preparing the book for printing, at no charge to us. In addition, our thanks are due to the many Kintbury people who have contributed articles, provided photographs or drawings, or spoken of their memories; this includes several people now living away from the village, who still feel part of our community and have given their help. Their names are listed in 'Acknowledgements' at the end of the book.

This is not a history book. We have made every effort to check accuracy, but human memory is not infallible. We are also conscious that in some instances more could be discovered of the subjects concerned. However, if this book evokes your memories or, as a newcomer, gives you a 'feel' for the life lived here this past hundred years, it will have served its purpose.

We send all our readers good wishes for the new century.

Sybil Flinn
Editor   October 1999

The Natural History of Kintbury

Location

Kintbury lies in the valley of the River Kennet. It is bounded to the north by the higher ground of the Lambourn Downs and The Ridgeway, beyond which lies the Vale of the White Horse. To the south there is the high ground of the North Hampshire Downs with Walbury Hill, Combe Gibbet and The Wayfarer's Walk. Walbury Hill is, at 297 metres, the highest chalk hill in England. The Wayfarer's Walk is a long distance footpath which winds its way through Hampshire to Emsworth, near the West Sussex border. Kintbury village is about 100 metres above sea level and it is sheltered by the higher ground to the north and south. The River, the Kennet and Avon Canal and the railway line from London to the West Country all pass just to the north of village habitation. The soil of the area is predominantly chalky which gives areas of traditional chalk downland, increasingly hard to find in recent years. There are small areas of acid heathland not far distant at Inkpen and Sole Common attracting flora and fauna which enjoy these conditions. The position of the village has resulted in the surrounding countryside containing many different habitats which attract a wide diversity of wildlife.

Habitats

Many Kintbury houses have extensive gardens and the conurbation is small enough so that nowhere is far from open fields. This has enabled many species of plants and animals, that can tolerate close proximity to man, to flourish in the village itself. The river and the canal on the north side provide different habitats that go with the different water flow rates. The river is famous for its trout fishing and the waters are carefully managed. This has given unpolluted, clear, fast-flowing water with managed water depths. The restrictions on public access have also allowed many species to prosper without being subjected to excessive human pressures. The canal has been opened up for pleasure use in recent years and the summer months see a steady flow of craft, most of them passing through at a sedate pace. The marshy areas close to the river and the canal both provide unique habitats.

Away from the water the land is fertile and predominantly flat so that it can be used for many different crops. There are large fields which are used for growing wheat while there are also pasture areas for cattle and sheep to graze. The area is well provided with woodland, most of which is actively managed for sporting purposes with pheasants being the main quarry although red-legged partridges are also reared. There are also areas where use has been made of government grants for land to be 'set aside'. With areas of common land and chalk downland not far away, there is an excellent range of habitats.

Birds

In spring, the area attracts many summer migrants. The chiffchaff is usually the first to arrive although some stay through the winter. The much rarer Cetti's warbler can also be found along the canal, usually between Green Lane and Brunsdon Lock. Nightingales nest locally in scrub along the canal and ospreys have been sighted, usually close to trout waters, when breaking their journey on their way to Scottish lochs. The cuckoo is another welcome spring visitor. Throughout the year kingfishers are frequently seen with several pairs nesting. Barn owls have become scarce nationally in recent years but this area of West Berkshire is still a stronghold for the species. For several years a pair have nested in an old ash tree behind Barton Court. Tawny owls make their presence known by much hooting in the late autumn as they encourage the young from the previous spring to go into the world and fend for themselves. A little owl can often be seen at Inglewood close to the stud farm. A few

Barn Owl

Mallard   *Coot*   *Tufted Duck*

years ago, the wet meadows between the village and Barton Court were left ungrazed during the summer months. This encouraged the grass to grow unusually long which enabled voles to flourish and this in turn attracted a number of short-eared owls which stayed through the winter. Skylarks are plentiful in areas of grassland at higher levels. The birds of prey are particularly notable. The red kite has been on the edge of extinction but a programme of reintroduction has been established by the RSPB and it appears that they have gained a toehold on the nearby North Hampshire Downs in the Combe and Faccombe areas. Kestrels are common, buzzards and sparrowhawks are regularly seen while merlin and hobby are less common visitors. In winter, redwings and fieldfares frequent most areas and golden plover and lapwings flock onto ploughed fields at Irish Hill and the fields bordering the Bath Road. Careful scrutiny of hedgerows and scrub may yield goldcrests and occasionally, the much rarer firecrest, while the wet areas attract herons, Canada geese and tufted ducks. The small stream by the railway bridge is home for water rails in the winter and when heavy rains cause the field behind Home Farm to flood, pochard, gadwall, widgeon and teal are welcome visitors. The colder weather also attracts finches such as siskins and bramblings. Rarer species such as crossbill, stonechat, woodcock and snipe are occasionally seen. During migration a few wheatears and whinchats are usually spotted as they pass through. The common sandpiper is another occasional visitor. It frequents the canal between

Water Rail

Brunsdon Lock and Lower Denford where it can be recognised by its habit of flying along the canal when disturbed and then alighting and waiting for the observer to approach with a bobbing action.

Flowers

Spring brings a splendid show of, firstly, snowdrops in the churchyard; these are closely followed by winter aconites at Inglewood and later daffodils and bluebells. Pussy willow and hazel catkins also announce that warmer days are on the way. The area is well catered for with orchids with the common spotted being easily found in Catmore Copse. The pyramidal, burnt tip, fragrant orchids and twayblades are all found at the nearby Ham Reserve. Early marsh orchids are present at Lower Denford and early purple orchids can be found near the road to Woolton Hill, just beyond Three-cornered Hat.

The crocus field at Inkpen provides an exceptional show with millions of blooms being cared for in this excellent nature reserve. How they came to this area is a mystery. Tradition has it that the plant was originally brought back by the Crusaders as a source of saffron for flavouring and colouring sweetmeats. However this particular crocus does not produce saffron!

The Canal provides a good opportunity for wild flowers to flourish and in the summer months there are displays of meadowsweet, purple loosestrife, hemp agrimony and rosebay willow herb. The rarer elecampane, sneezewort and skullcap are also present. There are many mature trees which have been growing for hundreds of years. Oak and beech are widespread and ash can also be found. There are few more splendid sights than that of the horse chestnuts at Barton Court in full blossom. At lower levels, blackthorn and elder have prospered and provide ample opportunity for locals to gather the fruit and flowers to make sloe gin and elderflower and elderberry wines.

Mammals

The numerous spinneys and coverts which are nurtured to give cover for pheasants also provide refuge to deer. Roe deer are widespread and require regular culling to control their numbers. Fallow deer are rarer and favour the quieter areas around Combe Gibbet. The introduced muntjac also enjoy the habitat and have become well established. Despite the attention of gamekeepers, foxes, stoats and weasels continue to hold their own. Grey squirrels maintain an on-going battle with villagers who put out peanuts: are they for squirrels or birds? The woods have enabled badgers to establish some large setts and they can be watched as the adults emerge to forage and the cubs to play on warm summer evenings. The larger arable fields provide an ideal environment for hares to prosper. They entertain with 'boxing antics' in the spring, hide in the lush undergrowth during the summer and then have their considerable numbers exposed as autumn and then winter denude the landscape. Water voles can be found along the canal although a loud 'plop' may be the only clue. The population of this 'Wind in the Willows' character has dropped in most parts of the country in recent years and Kintbury has suffered in line with other areas. It may be that the culprit is the mink which is present in small numbers and is vigorously pursued by the river keepers because of its liking for fresh trout.

Bats are thriving. Pipistrelles favour the buildings in the village while Daubenton's prefer to skim the waters of the river and the canal while searching for insects. The rarer and larger noctule bat can also be found close to the fields and trees of Barton Court.

Fish, crustaceans, amphibians and reptiles

The River Kennet is regarded as being among the best trout rivers in England. The canal is also well patronised by coarse anglers, and many large specimens have been caught. Surprisingly large freshwater crayfish flourish in the canal and river waters.

There is a small nature reserve with several ponds on the edge of the village. This is owned by The Berkshire, Buckinghamshire and Oxfordshire Naturalists Trust and it was established to preserve the environment for great crested newts. This is a Protected Species which thrives in the Kintbury habitat as do palmate and smooth newts. Grass snakes are occasionally seen while slow-worms are more common. There are also healthy populations of common frogs and toads.

Great Crested Newt

Illustrations for this chapter are by Valerie Shirley.

Butterflies and insects

All of the common butterflies can be found together with several rarer varieties. The purple hairstreak and white admiral enjoy the habitat of Catmore Copse with its established deciduous woods. Occasionally the silver washed fritillary is present. Comma, gatekeeper, ringlet and red admiral can be seen regularly. The chalk habitat enables the common blue and chalkhill blue to survive while the holly blue can also be found.

In the early autumn it is possible to find glow-worms during late evening walks along the canal and in a few other areas. The ponds attract several species of dragonfly with the emperor dragonfly and the common blue damselfly being most widespread.

In summary, Kintbury provides an excellent environment for many species of wildlife. The area contains several different habitats and the land is actively managed so that it will provide a home for many interesting and sometimes rare plants and animals for many years to come.

This review was compiled by Kintbury Wildlife Group which is an active organisation in the village with interest in the local environment and its wildlife.

What's about?

At the end of each meeting of the Kintbury Wildlife Group, the chairman asks the members "What's about?".

During the last twelve months, members have sighted all the birds and butterflies below. Some are very common; others very rare. How many have you seen – and have you any additions?

Birds

Blackbird	Greenfinch	Partridge, red-legged
Blackcap	Gull, black-headed	Pheasant
Bullfinch	Gull, lesser	Pipit, meadow
Bunting, reed	black-backed	Pipit, tree
Buzzard	Heron	Plover, golden
Chaffinch	Hobby	Redstart
Chiffchaff	Jackdaw	Redstart, black
Coot	Jay	Redwing
Cormorant	Kestrel	Robin
Crow	Kingfisher	Rook
Cuckoo	Kite, red	Sandpiper, common
Dove, collared	Lapwing	Sandpiper, green
Dove, stock	Linnet	Shelduck
Dove, turtle	Magpie	Siskin
Duck, tufted	Mallard	Skylark
Dunnock	Martin, house	Snipe
Fieldfare	Moorhen	Sparrow, house
Flycatcher, spotted	Nightingale	Sparrowhawk
Gadwall	Nuthatch	Starling
Goldcrest	Owl, barn	Swallow
Goldfinch	Owl, little	Swan, black
Goose, Canada	Owl, tawny	Swan, mute
Grebe, little	Partridge, grey	Swift

Tern, common
Teal
Thrush, mistle
Thrush, song
Tit, blue
Tit, coal
Tit, great
Tit, long-tailed
Tit, marsh
Tit, willow
Treecreeper
Wagtail, grey
Wagtail, pied
Wagtail, yellow
Warbler, Cetti's
Warbler, garden
Warbler, reed
Warbler, sedge
Warbler, willow
Water rail
Wheatear
Whinchat
Whitethroat
Whitethroat, lesser
Wigeon
Woodcock
Woodpecker, great spotted
Woodpecker, green
Woodpigeon
Wren
Yellowhammer

Butterflies

Admiral, red
Admiral, white
Brimstone
Blue, common
Blue, chalkhill
Blue, holly
Clouded yellow
Comma
Copper, small
Fritillary, silver-washed
Fritillary, dark green
Gatekeeper
Hairstreak, purple
Heath, small
Meadow brown
Orange tip
Painted lady
Peacock
Ringlet
Skipper, dingy
Skipper, large
Skipper, small
Speckled wood
Tortoiseshell, small
White, large
White, small
White, green-veined
White, marbled

Note: All sightings were within a five-mile radius from the centre of Kintbury.

The Parish Council

by Heather Turner

The first Parish Council in Kintbury was formed in 1895 as a result of the Local Government Act of 1894 which set up the system of County, District and Parish Councils, and which continues today in more or less the same form. Parish Councils took over many local duties previously administered by Parochial Church Councils or their appointees.

The new Kintbury Council met for the first time in January 1895 in the Schoolroom at St. Mary's School (now St. Mary's House). Nine Councillors were elected by poll and of these Mr. Francis Hobson Appach was elected Chairman. As no member was prepared to take on the duties of Clerk without pay, Mr. Job Buckeridge, Assistant Overseer of the Poor was appointed Clerk at an additional salary of £10 (to be reduced to £5 a year or two later) and he was to hold this job for over 30 years. Little else is recorded as having been discussed at this meeting...it took a while for the council to get into its stride!

Then, as now, elections took place every three years and so there was no election in 1900, but in 1901 and the Councillors elected then were:

Samuel Argyle	Thomas Bronsdon
Harvey Dodd	William Huw Dunn
John Cook Ewins	George Thomas Killick
John Barlow Page	Harold Edgar Phillips
Tom Witt.	

Mr. Dunn was elected Chairman and remained so for the next 10 years. These Councillors represented a good cross section of village life including such occupations as Brickmaker, Bootmaker, Clerk, Carpenter and 'Gentleman'. Council activities moved, as befitted the age, at a leisurely pace. Meetings were called about four times a year and decisions not made in a hurry. It was common for items raised, say, in the spring to be deferred until the autumn. Likewise something which cropped up in the autumn would very likely be left until the following spring. Anything deemed controversial was usually referred to a 'Parish Meeting' so that residents could be consulted. Elections were almost always decided by 'show of hands' at one of these Parish gatherings where the public could vote in nine members. Sometimes only nine people appeared to be present, usually the retiring councillors – who voted themselves back into office! However, there were times when as many as twenty-seven nominations were received and on one occasion those present had to be reminded that they could only vote for nine people. Casual vacancies tended to be filled by the councillors nominating suitable candidates. It seems that it was not until some time in the 30s that a 'proper' election was called for – the casual approach seeming to satisfy everyone. It is also interesting that no woman became a councillor until almost half way through the century and up to the present time very few have chosen to serve.

All early meetings were held at St. Mary's School but transferred to the Coronation Hall when this was built.

One of the first big decisions the Council had to take was whether Kintbury should have street lights. This was first suggested in 1897 and there appeared to be great enthusiasm. A 'public subscription' list was drawn up and the sum of £31 was promised towards the capital cost of £40 for installing sixteen lamps around the central part of the village. However, when put to the vote whether to proceed, the idea was rejected. Within a year though it was back on the agenda and this time approved and the lamp standards put in place. Running costs were estimated to be £15 a year, which included the lamplighter's wages of 6/- (30p) per week. These were oil lamps, for the village had neither gas nor electricity and the council had a thought for the ratepayers pocket as illumination was strictly controlled – lights only from October to March, dusk to 10p.m. and no lights at the full moon, or two days before and two days after! The Assistant Overseer to the Poor, and Parish Clerk you will remember, was asked to look after the Lighting Account: however this must have been the proverbial 'Straw' because he refused to take on this extra task without payment so a reluctant council offered him £5 a year, making his total salary for his various jobs £55 a year. The village kept its oil lamps until 1913 when a deal was struck with Harold Phillips, Mill Owner and 'Proprietor of the Electric Lighting Works' (a corrugated iron shed behind the Mill), to convert the lamps to electric power at an annual running cost of £26 per annum. Mr. Phillips continued to supply his electricity until 1931, when the Wessex Electricity Company took over at a significantly higher cost to the ratepayers. Today our village is lit dusk to dawn, summer and winter, and street lighting continues to be one of the main concerns of the Parish Council and is financed by a local special charge on our council tax bill.

The local water supply also came to the Council's attention early on. In 1900 Hungerford District Council invited Kintbury to join them in a scheme which would have brought us mains water. However this offer was turned down, it being stated that 'Kintbury was already supplied with good water' – from its various wells. Mains water came up again in 1922, but Hungerford got the same response. 'Kintbury already had a good supply' and it was not until 1931 that terms were agreed for a piped supply.

The state of footpaths came up regularly, especially those to Avington and Titcomb. These were used regularly then by workpeople, schoolchildren and people on their daily visit to the shops. Until 1946, when it became a County Council responsibility, the Parish looked after its own paths and was expected to maintain them, so they were regularly contracting with local tradesmen to carry out repairs, which they did with supplies of gravel hauled by horse and cart from local pits. In 1909 a dispute arose between the Council and a Kintbury contractor as to how many loads he had hauled in relation to those for which he charged, this being picked up on the Annual Audit. He was summoned to appear before the Council (the only recorded occasion of this happening) to explain himself. He produced his Carter as witness because he had 'counted the loads'. However it seems that his explanation was not accepted and a refund of just under £2 was made by him.

Roads were also an issue with regular complaints about holes and ruts. In the first part of the century roadmaking consisted mainly of tar poured over loose gravel to consolidate a surface and this was forever breaking up particularly in the winter months. Carts and traction engines regularly created ruts which had to be filled in and the road 'scraped' with a mechanical device designed for this purpose. This was the responsibility of Hungerford District Council who were always keen to be sure that they only treated 'public roads', and it is recorded that they once queried 'Withybed Road' – this being the road from Kintbury to Hungerford via the Common! As traffic increased, so the roads improved and by the 30s complaints seem to have disappeared. From early days the Council tried very hard to get Berkshire County Council to build a bridge over the railway because of the inconvenience of the level crossing. The County sympathised – but there was never enough money 'in this year's estimates' for it ever to become a reality. Likewise the Great Western Railway was urged to provide a passenger footbridge but this also fell on deaf ears. So, today we still have our level crossing, no footbridge and the potholes in the roads have returned.

Kintbury's 18th century Fire Engine cropped up regularly in the minutes. In 1896 the Council decided that it needed attention and called upon the firm of Merryweather in London to inspect and report upon its condition. This they did at length and it seems that nearly every part needed renewing and it would cost nearly £20 to put it right. They ended their report by saying that maybe it would be better to buy a new engine. It appears no action was taken and for the next 50 years its future was raised regularly – mostly as to which was the best way to dispose of it since 'it was of no use'. The engine was stored in various places including St. Mary's School, offered to Newbury Museum, who at that time were not interested, and finally one of the Councillors was given permission to dispose of it for scrap. However, Mr. Peter Hassell, a Newbury plumber, rescued it when it was on its way to the scrapyard and it is currently stored by Newbury Museum awaiting restoration, but with its true ownership somewhat obscure.

Kintbury's 18th century Fire Engine;
now in Newbury awaiting restoration.

Early days also saw the Council concerned with its drains and with 'soapy water' which seemed to get into its rainwater gulleys. There was also a posting of notices to deter those causing 'a nuisance' and the landlord of the 'Barley Mow' was requested to screen his urinal since users were 'visible from the street'.

During the First World War the Council met infrequently and their sole recorded effort was to set up a sub-committee to encourage the growing of food, but there is no mention of it ever meeting or doing anything. However it did have a hand in setting up a committee to organise a 'Peace Tea'– reported elsewhere – and also accepted an offer of 'War Trophies', suggesting these should be displayed in the Coronation Hall. I wonder whether they ever materialised and if so what happened to them!

In 1919 the Council turned its attention to the desperate need to improve living conditions in Kintbury by the building of new houses, referred to then as 'Council cottages'. This matter was referred to regularly over the next 25 years with houses being built gradually in small numbers at The Crescent, Holt Road and Burtons Hill during the 20s, and in the 30s at Laylands Green. Again after the Second World War many more were built. Some councillors did not agree with the sites used and suggested it would be better to build in the farming areas and on the outskirts of the village so that the men would be nearer to their work. Places mentioned were at Elcot, the Ash House (junction of Mill Lane with the A4), and the Templeton Road between Inglewood Lodge and Kintbury Farm.

In the 30s attention was given to the need for main drainage but the war intervened and so this did not reach Kintbury until 1948. More recent years have seen changes in matters discussed. The ownership of the Vicarage Bridge appeared regularly with all possible owners denying responsibility due to the extensive repairs needed.

Consequently it was eventually narrowed to a footpath but no repairs so far. In 1961 a new item appeared and this was consultation by the District Council on planning applications. Views are sought, but not always followed, a source of continuing concern with Councillors. Some items remain constant – footpaths and access to them, and lighting.

Many prominent local people have served on the Council over the century and its Chairmen have included the Rev. A. Edwards, Mr. A.S. Gladstone, Dr. Boulton and, in more recent times, Mrs. Doreen Anstey (the only woman Chairperson) and Mr. Tom Dyer. The present Chairman is Mr. Roger Groves. Clerks tended to serve for long periods and have included after Mr. Buckeridge, Mr. W. Hosken, Mr. H. Silcock, Mr. L. Gilbert, Mr. C. S. Drummond and our present Clerk, Mr. Chris Trigwell. Currently our Councillors, in addition to the Chairman are:

Mark Hooper	Tom Dyer
John Freedland	Angela Hall
Bert Newman	William Newton
Terry O'Neill	Keith Plank
Heather Turner	Michael English

making a total of eleven, two more than at the beginning of the century.

The first Council houses in Kintbury – The Crescent – built in the 1920s. Note the well for water, with sloping cover, and 'The Firs' in the background (left).

Digging up Newbury Street for the main drainage installation in 1948. One can see that Kintbury is indeed, built on chalk.

Life at the Vicarage

by Rev. Debby Plummer

Walking down Church Street, you meet a cluster of houses surrounding the churchyard, with names associated with the parish church. On your left there is Church House, home of the Chapman Pinchers; later, as the road sweeps round to the right of St. Mary's churchyard, you reach St. Mary's House; it was, for most this century, the village school, and was then run, until very recently, as a guest house by Alan and Margaret Barr. Follow the street until it ends and you are facing the elegant frontage of the Old Vicarage, built in 1860 to replace an earlier house on the site (where Jane Austen probably stayed during visits to Kintbury). This is where Robert Harris and his family now live. Turn left and follow the footpath uphill into the churchyard and, over the wall to your right, you will see the Vicarage which succeeded it. Built in 1938, on an acre of glebe land held back from the extensive vicarage gardens when the Victorian vicarage was sold, this dignified house held sway until 1994; it then became the private property of Gill Guy and took the name of 'The Old Rectory', one of the few possible names left! However, you need to hunt farther afield to find today's vicarage.

I moved into the brand-new vicarage at Elizabeth Gardens with my husband Jeremy in 1995. It is a spacious and practical 4-bedroomed house at the blind end of a small development of six homes, all built on the site where Mrs. Elizabeth Butler's bungalow stood. Her primulas and daffodils still break into flower in our garden, despite the upheaval they suffered in 1994. That means that there have been three vicarages serving Kintbury in the twentieth century. There was method in the madness: houses give strong messages about their occupants and what was appropriate for the Rev. Arthur William Henry Edwards, Vicar of Kintbury from 1886 until 1928, neither matches the lifestyle of Rev. Deborah Ann Plummer nor the expectations of today's parishioners. Allow me to draw you two sketches, from the very beginning and very end of the century, and I will leave you, gentle reader, to fill in the intervening years.

Arthur Edwards grew up in Ireland and was educated at Trinity College Dublin and Oxford. His distaste for the lack of respect in which the Irish churches held one another was to have a lifelong effect on his attitudes. In 1872 (aged 23) he was ordained and came to Kintbury the following year as curate, to work with the new vicar, William Fraser Campbell, a son-in-law of Lionel Oliver, patron of the living of Kintbury. Lionel was a close friend of the Dundas family of Barton Court and a regular visitor there and at the vicarage, where his daughter Georgina lived. Arthur met, courted and married Kitty (Catherine), Georgina's younger sister; this was a good marriage between two thoughtful people of compatible backgrounds and substantial wealth (recorded in a deed of settlement). From Kintbury, Arthur moved to a third curacy in Clewer just before the wedding. Two further curacies at Sevenoaks and Croydon, occupied the years until 1886, when the Vicar of Kintbury died unexpectedly and Lionel Oliver invited his other clerical son-in-law to replace him. So Arthur returned to Kintbury with his family and his long incumbency began.

Arthur and Kitty arrived in 1886 with four young children, a family rapidly augmented by Dorothy, Lionel and Agnes and completed by Frances in 1898. Kitty was busy with childbearing in the early days but helped by four servants, two washerwomen and a gardener. Arthur's unmarried sister, Mary, lived with them at Kintbury and threw herself into parish work with energy. A great-nephew remembers her as a 'large and rather forbidding figure', a memory tempered by family photographs.

Vicarage folk were gentry but far more importantly they ran the charitable centre and welfare state of Kintbury. The village people then were very poor and the Hungerford workhouse was universally dreaded. Mary, Margaret and Lina helped with coal and blanket clubs, with savings clubs (supplemented by local gentry) and at Mothers' Meetings. They ran the village library and organised 'Penny Readings' in the village school in those days before radio and newspapers. The vicar knew every parishioner and visited daily from 4-6 p.m. on foot, or by pony and trap to outlying areas. Kintbury is a large parish – seven miles between its north and south boundaries.

Arthur Edwards spent more than half his life in Kintbury. He and his family ministered stability and practical Christian charity for 42 years. He was undoubtedly a central figure in village life, with an acute mind, perceptive in dealing with people, and he was a man of his time, with gravitas and social ease. He and Kitty are commemorated in the chancel of St. Mary's church and their eight sons and daughters recorded in a framed inscription near the organ; the green chasuble, paschal candlestick and a chalice and paten were given in their memory. Mary seems to have no memorial, so let this chapter be hers!

How different life is today in Kintbury and at the vicarage in many ways! The twentieth century has irreversibly altered rural life. There are plenty of people still here whose forebears lived in Kintbury in 1900 but many others have chosen it as a commuter base or retirement home. The population has grown from 1655 in 1900AD to nearly 3000 in 2000AD. On the whole the extreme poverty has gone. We have plenty of deprivation here, however, and the vicar is still involved behind the scenes in helping to alleviate it. Nowadays, since the establishment of a Welfare State, clergy work in close partnership with Citizens Advice Bureau, counselling organisations, local charities, social services, health centre, Notrees and volunteer groups to make sure that real needs are met. We never get it all right – there are always some people who fall through all the nets – so we are constantly looking and listening out for the gaps.

In this very private culture, less people come knocking on my door. Some of them are wayfarers, tramping the countryside, usually with a history of addictions, failed relationships and sometimes mental illness; they always go away fed, equipped and cleaned up (if they wish!) and I, Jeremy or a churchwarden organises them a bed for the night, often at St. Petroc's in South Newbury. Other visitors are children and young people, just dropping in for half an hour or so. Yet others come on church business – or to talk in depth about their experience of God – or for counselling. Not all of these people will be from Kintbury (similarly, not all Kintbury people talk to me): it is often helpful to talk about very private matters away from your home parish.

Visiting is rewarding and enjoyable and I never have as much time as I would like for it: in this busy village, with over 30 clubs and societies, it is good to visit people where they meet as well as at home. It is no longer necessary for a vicar, wife or sister to run everything but good to encourage and support all neighbourliness, all creative enterprises and everything that gives people value. It is impossible in a village of nearly 3000 inhabitants (with considerable turnover) for the vicar to know everyone or be at every event but it is possible for a vicar to be a leading team player, a community builder and community analyst as well as community theologian. I take writing a monthly letter in 'The Fisherman' very seriously and find it a great privilege to preach at services – nearly half the village comes through our church doors each year, even in this secular age, for some purpose.

Contemporary clergy have many more calls on their time than Arthur Edwards had. In the last year, as well as pastoral work, school involvement and running services, I have helped to organise a youth mission, organised a conference for clergy, fostered relationships with other Christian churches and been a guest speaker on many occasions. Even services are more challenging these days: it is important to maintain the time-honoured trio (Matins, Evensong and Holy Communion) from the Book of Common Prayer but many people prefer to worship in dignified modern language. So we also include the contemporary versions of these services, plus ecumenical services, services for Remembrance Sunday, Rogation Day, Mothering Sunday, Christian Aid Week, Marriage Renewal, memorial services for bereaved relatives, healing services, quiet days & retreats, Family services, 'Songs of Praise', children's and youth services and much more! It is my desire that we meet people wherever they are and help them to progress along the Christian road towards greater humaness and greater godliness.

Church life has changed in other ways too. In the 1990s Kintbury has had a woman curate, Pat Gillham, and now has a woman as its parish priest: it was the first parish in Newbury Deanery to appoint a woman vicar, so hats off to Kintbury! This ends the century in which so many doors have been opened to women – the vote, university degrees and access to equal opportunities at work – and every role in our church life can now be taken by men and women alike, whether it be flower-arranger, musician, churchwarden, altar server or parish priest. How long will it be before we have woman who are diocesan bishops, like New Zealand?

Behind the scenes, decision-making has changed radically. In Arthur Edwards' time, the individual patron (Lionel Oliver) could appoint his son-in-law without consultation. That is rare now in the Church of England. Now Kintbury's priest is chosen by the Bishop of Oxford or by the Oxford Diocesan Board of Patronage (they take it in turns): the parish is consulted first and the churchwardens take part in the interview process. Everyone in the parish had a chance to meet me and the other candidates in 1994 and to pass on their impressions: so this was a truly collaborative experience. Our routine decision-making is just as collaborative, with the Parochial Church Council sharing responsibility for many areas of church life and with committees and working parties taking care of mission, children and youth provision, worship, communication and the church building, churchyards and finance. In other words, we are a contemporary church meeting in an ancient and venerable church building.

I end by summarising my hopes and dreams for Kintbury and its parish church, St. Mary the Virgin. May this village be neighbourly but respectful of privacy, watchful of its vulnerable people, tough in combating prejudice and gossip, generous and socially conscious in global as well as local issues, and may its people strike a balance between work and play, between health of body, mind, spirit and relationships.

May our church be a homely house, open to all, offering dignified and approachable worship, a 'family' atmosphere and an authentic spiritual life. God bless Kintbury and all who live, visit and work here!

St. Mary's Church –

A Century of Change and Preservation

by Thora Morrish

When the century began the Church of St. Mary's had recently undergone two restorations and been officially reopened by the Bishop of Oxford. The building, apart from a few minor alterations or additions since, therefore looked much as it does now. The restorations were severe but typical of what was going on in the country throughout the Victorian period. Nevertheless the church as we know it still has much of the original Norman building. The bases of the walls are Norman, as is the lofty chancel arch and the two doorways, south and west. The 19th century restorers removed all the windows that had been added over the years and replaced them with the present ones; the one exception was that in the north transept, which is original, but not the glass, of course. They also raised the roof, boarded it within and gave it the painted decorations which are such a feature of the church.

Old buildings, however, require constant care and maintenance and in this century there were four buildings that demanded the attention of the Parochial Church Council. To take them in alphabetical order, the first is *Avington*. Between 1931 and 1949 negotiations went on to unite the two benefices – finally accomplished after the consent of George VI in Council was given – and the old rectory at Avington was pulled down. Then in 1981, Lord Howard de Walden took over the church at Avington, this time with Queen Elizabeth II's consent. But the people of Kintbury have not lost contact with the old church, for Lord Howard welcomes them to services on many occasions throughout the year.

Secondly, another church – *Christ Church*. This was built in 1867 at Kintbury Crossroads on land given by the Earl of Craven to meet the needs of the many people who lived in that area, and to be a chapel for the new cemetery adjoining. However, in 1946 the church was declared structurally unsafe and demolished.

Next is the *Parish Room* in Station Road. It was given by Mr. A. S. Gladstone in 1939 and was held by Trustees on behalf of the church. For many years it was a great asset – all P.C.C. meetings were held there, the County Council used it as a base for its lending library; Lent lunches, discussion groups, Brownies, etc. used it. But repairs and decorations and proper heating were all necessary. The Men's Fellowship did yeoman work on decorating and minor repairs, but the number of lettings, which meant income, went down and down, and finally the building was

Christ Church.

sold and became a private house.

Lastly, there is *St. Mary's Room*. When the school was moved to Gainsborough Avenue, 'The Limes' – former home of the headmaster – was sold and the money used to build St. Mary's Room in 1980. This room, attached to St. Mary's Church, is now in constant use. It could have been larger save for the local authority, who insisted on very deep foundations at great expense, stating "the soil had been disturbed". So it had – by the Anglo Saxons some hundreds of years before!

In 1957 the 5-yearly 'Inspection of Churches' was introduced which certainly saved some old buildings from falling into decay. Not in Kintbury. Heating being of paramount importance, the old solid fuel boiler was replaced by an oil model in 1963 which, with perfect timing, split beyond repair a few days before Christmas in 1987. An entirely new system of hot-air heating fuelled by propane gas was eventually installed in 1991, Kintbury being the first church in Berkshire to adopt this system. Both the chancel and nave roofs were retiled, the tower roof was done in asphalt and the west face was re-rendered when the original flints were discovered and used.

Alterations to the interior of the church were not very major ones but nevertheless at the time created controversy. In 1956 the east window had its sill lowered by 30 centimetres, so that the window was back to its original and proper proportions. The 19th century stained glass was removed, but stored, and the window re-glazed

St. Mary's Church.

in plain glass, effecting a wonderful improvement to light inside the church. In 1972, the reredos behind the altar, was repainted by the prestigious firm of Campbell, who had worked at Westminster Abbey; Mr. Campbell himself coming to explain the religious significance of the colour used. In 1977 the wooden screen was moved from the chancel arch to the south transept, with a new top carved by Prof. Milnes-Walker, so that it filled this space. In 1986 the screen was glazed, so making the south transept a self-contained area for small gatherings and private prayer. The moving of the screen meant that the congregation could not only see the altar, but communion could be celebrated there. The oak gates at the south entrance of the churchyard being beyond repair, were replaced by iron ones. The organ was overhauled and repairs made to the interior of the tower. These changes cost money and there were constant and varied money-raising efforts. But with two energetic appeals and help from the Historic Churches Fund, the money was found.

Then in 1986 the situation changed, for in that year the Friends of St. Mary's was formed as a charitable trust and took over the burden of maintaining the fabric of the church. In a few years they raised £200,000 and by 1992 their efforts became evident. The chancel was re-roofed, the walls lime-washed and the ceiling repainted; while the whole church was re-wired and new lighting installed. The following year the nave was redecorated and the ceiling splendidly repainted. In 1994 St. Mary's Room was given a new pitched roof instead of the flat one which leaked, and in 1995 major structural work was done to the north

transept. The Friends are now engaged in extensive repairs to the fabric of the tower, while an Access Committee is undertaking various improvements for those with disabilities: a loop for the hard-of-hearing, a sound system and alteration of levels to enable wheelchair access from the west door.

To conclude this brief survey of the church in the last hundred years, here are a few events which are of importance. In 1994 the churchyard was finally declared closed for burials, although space is allocated for the interment of ashes. After many discussions with the archdeacon, the Reverend R. Birt, the P.C.C. decided to use the Alternative Service Book, keeping the 1662 Prayer Book for certain services. A Free Will Offering Scheme was introduced and the parish magazine 'The Fisherman' started by the Reverend Martin Jones, which today provides an excellent guide to most happenings in Kintbury. And we were burgled! We lost a table that held books, a silver candlestick from Jerusalem, the carpet in front of the altar, and the Darrell 16th century helmet from the south transept.

On a more cheerful note, the church has had several gifts – an embroidered panel of village features on the south wall of the nave was worked by members of the congregation to celebrate St. Mary's 1,000th birthday in 1993; a gold threadwork Victorian altar frontal was completely restored by Mrs. Margaret Moore and is used for church festivals; and there are other small gifts in good use. We aim to keep the church in what the rural dean called 'good nick'.

A Vicarage Childhood

by Lina Edwards

In 1886 we moved to Kintbury where father was Vicar. What a change! A large house and garden with two lawns, one sloping down to the river where we had a boat.

Mother was as usual expecting, but we weren't told anything till the baby, Dorothy, arrived. There was a yard with stables and a pony, a crowd of hens and ducks, three cows and a pig. But above all there was Langford! He was a skilled gardener, and was looked up to by all the head gardeners of the neighbourhood. We took it all for granted, but now I look back with amazement at all he did. He managed the large kitchen garden and daily brought in a large vegetable basket. He kept flowers going in the garden and in beds on the lawn. He was a beemaster and kept four hives going. He managed and milked three cows and saw to their calving. He looked after the pig and saw to her farrowing. He cleaned out the stables and fed the pony. And in haysel time, he hired and took the leading place among the mowers (there were no machines). He saw to the hay in the upper field and in the two rented water meadows below the canal bridge, and yet he was always ready to make us whistles of horse chestnut, or bows and arrows and crusaders swords. He showed us all the birds nests in the shrubbery and in the garden. I could go now to the dunnock's, a wren's, a goldfinch's or blue tit's nest in an old pump. In fact he gave us our education in country life, which created *observation* which so many lack. Dear Langford, and all this he did for £1 a week! The garden was *his* garden, and all the help he ever got was a boy to pull, while he pushed the mowing machine once a week.

The first summer at Kintbury was *wonderful* to us four little townie children. We did our little bits of lessons in the morning and then we were free to go where we liked and do what we liked. We paddled in the edge of the river. We played in the hay. We took our mugs to the cowshed and Langford milked one of the cows into them, till the frothy milk made us white moustaches. We picked all sorts of wild flowers; kingcups and milkmaids, hogbeam and ragged robin. There was a laundry where two women came from the village and washed our clothes in big square wooden tubs. When we got our white socks dirty with mud from the river, we would run in to them, and they would change them for us and give us nice clean ones.

Mother was too busy settling in to the new home and looking after the new baby to worry much about us, and by degrees we settled down. There was no High School for us to go to, so she was determined that come what may we should learn languages, so Arthur was sent off at nine to a school in Hunstanton (near Heacham where our Oliver grandparents lived) and a Swiss governess came au pair and taught us *everything* in French. After a year or two she departed, and mother got a German, who taught us everything in German – so that I grew up knowing more of Moliere and Goethe, than I ever knew of Shakespeare!

Aunt Mary threw herself into parish work, and we children got to know the village. Things were very different then – the people were so poor. A whole set of little covered baskets were hung up in the back passage, so that little bits of pudding or a bowl of soup or whatnot could be taken to an invalid. There were the milk children who used to gather at the back door at 8 o'clock every morning and get their cans filled with skim milk, for separators had not been invented, and the cream was skimmed off the great pans of milk in the dairy and set aside for churning into butter once a week. This skim milk was very nourishing and mothers of big families were glad to have it. Then there were the 'Baby Baskets' with everything necessary for both mother and baby for a month (including a bar of soap for washing the things before bringing them back).

The Vicarage, Kintbury.

We visited in the village, we helped in the Sunday School. We managed the library – £5 worth of books were bought every year and school children paid 3 pence a quarter and borrowed books once a week. I think that library was very valuable – we all got a lot from the 'Boys Own Annual', Henty's books of adventure, and a set of books that came out yearly; Stories of Old England, Stories of America and so on. We read them all, and we gradually expanded our natural history researches. We kept tadpoles and minnows; we had a tortoise. We collected birds' eggs, and butterflies and moths, and Aunt Mary gave us books that helped. We collected fossils and Arthur and I even skinned and stuffed a starling!

We quickly learnt to manage the boat and ranged up and down the river and canal, and, of all wonders, we got a Welsh pony of our own! Mother rode on father's pony and taught us to ride. We later got a 4-wheeled basket carriage and learnt how to catch the pony – she lived in the field – and to harness her. We drove all over the country and up on the downs to Inkpen Beacon. Arthur and I were taught to fish by Uncle Lionel on one of his visits from India. Certain things stick in my mind: I can see myself standing in a pink cotton frock (I must have been about 12) at about 7 on a summer morning, under the canal bridge, fishing for perch when a kingfisher came flying through the bridge and perched on the tip of my rod. He stayed there for a minute or two, while I held my breath – and the thrill I got has lasted the rest of my life!

I *must* put down another adventure – I learnt to tickle trout! One day, I found a large trout lying close up to a wooden fence that bordered a stream, so I tickled it under its tummy and it seemed to like it. I gradually worked up till I got my hands beneath its heaviest part, and then I heaved it suddenly out on to the bank. We were rather afraid of Braxton, the keeper, and well we might be, so we wrapped the fish in grass and trotted home with it in my pinny. Father looked grave and said it was *poaching*. He said the only thing to be done was for us to take the fish down to Barton Court and ask for Mr Winthrop and confess. So we wrapped it up and put it in a basket and trudged off, feeling awful, but it had to be done. We rang the bell and a terrifying butler came to the door: "Please can we see Mr Winthrop?", "No I'm sorry but he's away from home, would you like to leave a message?". "No thank you, it's not important" said I with a very thankful heart, and we turned grandly and walked down the steps. But didn't we skip and rejoice when he shut the door. When we got home, father decided that least said soonest mended, and we had the trout for lunch next day (poached).

When the Oliver grandparents died we were a little better off. I think that the Queen Anne's bounty which had been borrowed to build the house in 1860 was also paid off, so with a growing family two attic bedrooms were made for the servants, and their large bedroom was turned into a schoolroom. A new window was made on the south side and we pursued our studies there, instead of working at a table in the dining room window.

All this time our interest in natural history increased. We ranged all over the woods and fields with no one to say us nay. We helped with all the parish charities, there were many of them – the coal club, the blanket club, the Mother's Meetings (3 of them) – where women could finger over patterns from Pryce Jones, of flannels and sheetings, and pay for them by weekly payments. Then there was the Sunday School club where children could pay in 3d. or 4d. a week, till Advent Sunday when the cards were made up and a bonus added. The cards were signed by father, and could be taken to certain shops in Newbury, and the next Sunday the proud owner would appear in a new frock or coat. These clubs made a lot of work for the parson and his children. Father persuaded all the local gentry to subscribe to them so that every card had bonus added to it for regular payments, and every family that pinched a 4d. or 6d. out of the weekly wages, had a good hefty load of coal for the winter, or a couple of warm blankets. Mind you, coal cost only one shilling a hundredweight in those days! The other value of those clubs was that the parson knew everybody in the village intimately, and so did we. Father went out in his trap to visit the distant hamlets (Kintbury parish was 7 miles long). He spent every evening from 4 to 6 visiting in the village. I trudged off to Elcot with Aunt Mary across the fields for a Mother's meeting (3 miles) every week in the winter afternoons. We were very welcome with our reading aloud of a story book, and then a short piece out of some 'good book'. Life was pretty hard and there were no entertainments, no telly, no radio, no newspaper.

We got up all sorts of 'Penny Readings' at which the gentry paid 2/6d. Then there were a few one shilling seats, and the whole of the back of the school was filled with people who only paid one penny.

Editor's note: Caroline Edwards (1878 – 1972), always known in the family as Lina, was the second eldest of the Rev. Edwards' eight children. After her childhood in Kintbury, she became a teacher at 18 and in her early 20s fulfilled her ambition by being accepted for missionary work in India, where she was to spend her whole working life. We are very grateful to her nephew, Mr. John Edwards, for permission to quote from Lina's memoirs, written in her old age, but recalling so vividly childhood, as it was for the more privileged children in the early part of this century.

The Bells of St. Mary's and their ringers

by Adam Rae-Smith, Ringing Master

Bells have been associated with religious and ceremonial events for thousands of years throughout the world. The first mention of bells in Kintbury is over 400 years ago when the Commissioners' Inventory of 1552, in the reign of Edward VI recorded – *Kintbury iiij belles in the steple and a saunce bell...a sakaring belle*. The oldest bell now in the tower dates from 1576, and a further five date from 1629 to 1702. In 1995 St. Mary's reached a full octave, when two new bells were blessed at a special ceremony attended by H.M. Queen Elizabeth II.

An old medieval legend predates all records. It tells of the 'Great Bell' accidentally dropping into the Kennet on its return after re-casting. After many attempts to retrieve it failed, the local wizard advised yoking a team of twelve white heifers with a bright new chain, driven at midnight by twelve maidens, in complete silence lest the charm be broken. It was too much for one spectator, who cried, "Here again comes Kintbury Great Bell, In spite of all the devils in Hell!" The chain snapped and the bell rolled back into the river, where it is still reputed to be. Members of the local band have tried without success to locate it with metal detectors. It seems improbable that it would have been left there – in the last resort bell metal can be broken up easily.

Bells, like all mechanical objects, need attention and repair. This is well documented in the Parochial Church Council (P.C.C.) minutes, and the costs over the century make interesting reading. In 1884 the bell hangers Whites of Appleton, who have been associated with the Kintbury bells for over 100 years, re-hung the bells with new fittings. The total cost was about £80, with £60 donated by members of the Fowle family. Forty years later, in 1922, Whites re-hung the then six bells in a new oak frame for a cost of £197. Inflation had taken its toll by the time Whites returned in 1982 to re-bush and anneal the clappers at a cost of £478. Three years later, in 1985, the floor of the ringing chamber was replaced at a cost of £1,168. This was very necessary – the floor had become noticeably springy in the centre of the chamber, where a small table was placed to avoid anyone plunging through!

By the late 1980s it was clear that a major overhaul would soon be needed, and after obtaining several independent reports and estimates of £17,250 upwards, the P.C.C. committed themselves to the re-hanging in 1988. The newly formed Friends of St. Mary's raised £9,000 before other essential repair works were highlighted by the church architect's five-yearly inspection. These repairs were to cost over £125,000, and naturally took precedence. Although this meant the target for the bell hanging could not be met in 1988, the bell ringers were not defeated. They continued their own efforts, raising a further £18,500 by 1994. During this time, it was found a new cast iron two-bell frame could be bolted on to the side of the old oak frame at no extra cost. This was because the work could now be classed as an alteration to a listed building, and thus free from V.A.T. Interestingly enough, it was then discovered that 60 years previously the churchwarden, Mr. A.S. Gladstone, had attempted to add two new bells in this fashion to celebrate King George V's Silver Jubilee. Sadly, it failed as when the architect went into the belfry to draw up plans, he discovered that the roof was in a dreadful state, requiring £185 to repair.

When the decision to install the new frame was made in 1991, it was anticipated that the two extra bells could be added at a later date. However, in fact this provided the spur to a very successful appeal run in 1994 by Mrs. Billee Chapman Pincher, which raised over £30,000. Her brilliant idea was to dedicate one of the new bells to the memory of the jockey and trainer Sir Gordon Richards, who spent the later part of his life in Dove House in the High Street, and who had been a devout churchgoer. The Sir Gordon Richards Bell Appeal was launched and directed at the horse-racing fraternity – owners, trainers, jockeys, bookmakers, racecourses and all others, interested in the sport, and the appeal had a magnificent response. Meanwhile I decided to donate the new treble bell. This records the twelve names of the band at the time, together with an engraved photograph of my two Jack Russell terriers, Puffin and Toaster. As far as is known, this is the only bell to include dogs in its dedication.

The Royal Family was closely associated with the 1995 re-hanging. The Queen, the Queen Mother, the Prince of Wales and Princess Michael of Kent all contributed generously to the Sir Gordon Richards Appeal. The Queen had indicated that she would like to attend the blessing by Kintbury's new vicar, Debby Plummer, and so on March 28th the newly cast bells were ready on a velvet covered platform for the first official visit to Kintbury by a reigning sovereign.

Although the ceremony only lasted twenty five minutes, it required a great deal of planning and hard work beforehand. The church was cleaned from top to bottom – the windows for the first time in living memory! About 225 people were crowded into the church an hour before the Queen arrived, and kept engaged by choir music and singing hymns. Outside, the schoolchildren formed an avenue alongside the newly gravelled path. The whole village was caught up in the excitement of the visit, with the baker making bell shaped cakes and bread, and the potter commemorative plates and mugs. The event was given eight minutes on Meridian Television evening news. The work itself did not end until September, when it was celebrated by a evening concert attended by Princess Michael of Kent, followed by a dedication service on Sunday.

The Queen's visit, March 28th 1995

Although bells are nowadays thought of as part of the religious fabric and activity of the church, this has not always been the case. Traditionally, bell ringers were an unruly and drunken lot, ringing the bells as much for secular as religious occasions. It was only in Victorian times that vicars and rectors decided to assert their authority over the ringers. This was done in various ways, including the 'if you can't beat 'em, join 'em' missionary strategy which resulted in a large number of the clergy becoming very proficient ringers. Elsewhere, ropes were lengthened and ringing chamber floors removed so that the ringers had to ring inside the church itself, and were no longer able to sup their ale unseen in the tower. Kintbury fortunately escaped this treatment and the current band of ringers has revived the old traditions with their own wine rack in the ringing chamber holding their elderberry and other home made wines. As far as we know, Kintbury is unique in this respect!

As recently as thirty years ago, ringers were paid annually for their ringing, and were classed along with the verger, sexton and organist as church servants. Again the P.C.C. minutes reflect this relationship, and show that as much time was spent discussing this 'servant problem' as was the time given to finding money for the maintenance and repair of the bells. Sometimes the bells were not rung because ringers were not available or seemingly not tempted by the payment of £10 per annum fixed in 1921 and remaining in force until after the end of the Second World War.

A hundred years ago, the ringers were all men, and the band would have been a closed group open by invitation only. The First World War saw women encroaching on traditionally male preserves, including bell ringing, but not in Kintbury! Indeed, as late as 1958, when more ringers were needed, "Mr. Elridge asked if ladies could ring bells, and was informed that it was quite usual". Even so, it was not until 1963 when Gwenda Smith (who still rings at St. Mary's) became the first lady ringer in the band, having learnt to ring elsewhere.

Appropriately enough, the Thatcher era saw a new broom in 1984 with the appointment of Helen Weavers as the first woman to be Tower Captain of Kintbury. Helen modernised ringing at Kintbury, by introducing a style known as 'method ringing' which allowed more variety and enabled peals of three hours to be rung without repetition or impossible feats of memory. Until this time, the ringers had rung with cards on the floor in front of them, which told them which bell each should follow in turn. The ringing standard of the band improved steadily from this point on. In 1990, a milestone was reached, with the first three hour peal to include ringers from the Kintbury band. In 1995, the band won the local Oxford Diocese Newbury Branch striking competition for the first time. Finally, in 1998, Kintbury gained its own official and very musical method – Kintbury Surprise Major, composed by Geoff Dodd of Highclere.

One of the best aspects of bell ringing is the fraternity which exists – bell ringers come from all walks of life, and they can walk into a tower anywhere in the country on a practise night or Sunday, sure of a good welcome. As with other activities, however, disagreements and personality conflicts inevitably arise. There are plenty of tales of ringers in other towers who have taken offence without any provocation and disappeared never to be heard of again. We are very fortunate in Kintbury to have avoided this type of friction. The current set of ringers enjoy each other's company very much, and have earned a reputation as the friendliest and most social and cohesive band in the area. Long may it remain so!

Kintbury's Schools

Kintbury St. Mary's School

The National Society says that in 1833 Abstract of Education shows that a daily school under the management of the clergyman's daughter was commenced in Kintbury in 1831. It appears that this was held in what is now Barn Cottage in Station Road next to what was the Maid Marion Stores. The village school proper was built in 1870, just below the church, by the then vicar of Kintbury the Rev. J.W.D. Dundas, and remained so for the next 97 years. It is now a private dwelling called St. Mary's House and has a preservation order on it, which means that the external appearance must be maintained in the original Victorian style. The school log books provide a fascinating view of school life throughout the century. In the beginning St. Mary's was divided into Infants and Mixed Schools, each with its own Head Teacher. Children transferred to the Mixed School at the age of about seven and most remained there until the official leaving age of fourteen. However those boys and girls aged 12 and approaching their 13th birthday who had reached a certain standard were given a leaving certificate and were then free to go into employment. A surprising number did this, presumably in order to help family incomes. This practice stopped due to a change in legislation round about 1920. It is not recorded when Infant and Mixed schools amalgamated under one Head but it was probably before the First World War.

Log books record a very considerable amount of illness of children, one epidemic seeming to follow another and this included a particularly nasty bout of scarlet fever early in the century. These illnesses caused the closure of the school often by order of the Medical Officer. Sickness plus bad weather caused low attendances. Parents just did not send children in wet weather or wintery conditions – very probably due to inadequate clothing. Children including infants sometimes had to walk long distances to school – for instance from Avington, Clapton and Elcot.

Physical conditions within the school were poor by today's standards but reflected the age. Lavatories were separate from the main building and of the bucket variety, remaining so until well after the Second World War when main drainage came to the village. Heating was totally inadequate – coke stoves augmented later by radiators in some rooms. On cold days in winter on many occasions temperatures did not rise above the 30s farenheit and despite improvememts made in the thirties this situation continued to some extent almost throughout the life of the old school. Also, again until the early 'thirties there was no mains water, the school being served by a well and pump situated in the playground. Even when the new supply was laid on, it was only to one tap in the playground.

Despite these conditions, reports from H.M. Inspectors throughout the years were consistently good. However

St. Mary's School Football Team 1936 outside the old school.

from early times they constantly complained about the conditions under which the Infants were taught where some had to be seated on unsuitable desks on a gallery in one of the rooms and it was not until the middle thirties that this situation was remedied and other improvements made.

Early years provided only one significant event and this was quite a serious fire in 1906 which disrupted the school for 3 weeks, causing the infants to be transferred up the road to the Working Men's Club (now part of 23 Church Street). There was to be another quite serious fire in 1932 badly damaging one classroom and part of the roof.

Around this time the Headmaster (Mr. Packer) reported at length in the Log Book on the start of a 'Garden Project' on land loaned behind the school – now the garden of St. Mary's House and gardening was to form part of the curriculum for many years to come. Lots of problems occurred over the attendance of boys and girls at the Hungerford Practical Subjects Centre for Woodwork and Cookery respectively. These included transport not turning up, the Centre failing to tell the school that classes had been cancelled, leaving Kintbury children stranded in Hungerford and having to walk back and also disciplinary problems which on occasion resulted in the Headmaster going to Hungerford to 'sort things out'. All these were made more difficult because the school had no telephone so there were constant telegrams flying backwards and forwards updating situations. However, between the wars the school thrived, winning honours for sports, a reputation for strict regime and maintaining a good standard of teaching which survives to the present day.

Little is recorded about St. Mary's in wartime but the Newbury Weekly News reported in 1900 that Mr. Argyle, Headmaster, on getting news through a friend of the Relief of Ladysmith (Boer War) announced this to the children who then sang the National Anthem and paraded round the village spreading the good news. No records are available for the school during the First World War but the late Emily Newman remembered going with other children down to the Convalescent Hospital at Barton Court to help in the kitchens.

The Second World War brought evacuees, some in single families and a party of sixty from Dagenham, accompanied by their teachers who stayed here for about eighteen months. These were accommodated separately in the Methodist Schoolroom and also for a while in the Vestry of St. Mary's Church. By mid 1942 most returned home but those who remained were absorbed into St. Mary's School. Here Air Raid drills and gas mask inspections occurred regularly and the church was used as an Air Raid shelter, it being considered safer than the school because the children could take cover underneath the pews! The school did its bit for the war effort. Salvage items were collected, blackberries were picked for the Jam Factory (outbuildings at Inglewood Lodge), rose hips were gathered and the boys went to help with the potato harvest.

By 1947 the school had resettled into its peacetime regime but changes were on the way. In the Autumn of that year all children over the age of 13 were transferred to the Hungerford Secondary School. This released classroom space and made teaching activities easier. The following years saw many changes. Up to then virtually all lessons were in the classroom but the log book records many visits to films, industries, farms and other places of interest. School kitchens were built and children living at a distance were bussed to school.

By 1955, the church could no longer afford the upkeep of the building, so the school was taken over by Berkshire County Council and became a 'controlled' denominational school. In practice this means that the school is administered as a normal county primary school but the church retains its religious connection and incumbent is a member of the school governors. As a direct result of this administrative change, a unique development took place, of great interest to staff and children alike. For the first time in the history of the school flush lavatories were installed. In 1956 whilst a drainage trench was being dug in the school playground, workmen uncovered a large quantity of very old bones. These were sent to the British Museum and they were found to be the bones of Saxon men, women, children, red deer and dogs. In September 1956 the final step was taken to re-organise St. Mary's as a Primary School when children aged 11+ were transferred to Hungerford Secondary School. In January 1963 following the closure of Christ Church School on the southern edge of the village children were transferred to St. Mary's, the increase in numbers adding to congestion within the old school premises.

By 1967 conditions in the old school building had become rather difficult. It was overcrowded and had only the original small playground and no playing field: the accommodation was so poor that an overflow class had to be based in the Coronation Hall. After much campaigning, Berkshire County Council agreed to build the present school on land donated by Miss W. Lawrence. In January 1968, although work was still proceeding, the staff and children moved into the present school. For the first term, as the kitchen was not ready for use, lunches were cooked at the old school and brought up by taxi each day.

The active building programme in Kintbury caused the

Kintbury St. Mary's School Head Teachers	
1895 – 1906	Mr. S. Argyle
1906 – 1924	Mr. E. Wilde
1924 – 1945	Mr. E. Packer
1945 – 1946	Mr. T. Osborne (Acting)
1946 – 1954	Mr. J. Bull
1954 – 1978	Mr. F. Parry
1978 –	Mr. T. Dillon

number on roll to grow to the point that Berkshire County Council provided two temporary terrapin classrooms on the junior playground in 1976/78. These were 'relocated units' from a science block at a secondary school. By 1993 their condition had deteriorated to the extent that roof supports were fitted and they had to be evacuated when high winds were forecast! In 1993 the County agreed to replace the terrapins with more modern temporary rooms. The school conducted a feasibility study to see what a permanent extension would cost and the County agreed to do this, provided the school could find the difference between the two costs. The P.T.A. took it on as an objective. It was a massive challenge, but through hard work and tremendous support from all the parents, the difference was raised by numerous fund raising events within the time scale.

In 1994 work started on the extension to the school and the two new classrooms, a medical/group work room and boys' toilet came into use in September 1995.

The Miss Lawrence Trust has always been most supportive to the school and in 1998 provided a grant to establish a computer area for the older children. The school plays an active part in the Newbury Education Business Partnership and through this connnection a number of computers have been provided by Vodafone PLC. Action plans are in hand to link the school to the National Grid for Learning, Internet access and moving into the Millennium.

Kintbury St. Mary's School P.T.A. was formed in 1965 and became a registered charity in 1995. It has always been a very active organisation and has maintained a programme of educational and social evenings and over the years has raised large amounts of money to provide extra resources and facilities for the children. The P.T.A. has helped considerably to bring together people with a common interest – their school.

Christ Church School

This Church of England School was built in the latter part of the last century to serve the needs of the southern part of Kintbury and so it drew children from the Blandys Hill and Laylands Green areas as well as some from nearby Inkpen – particularly as the present Inkpen Junior School had not been built then and the former Inkpen School was at the other end of the village. Even so it is puzzling why it was located where it was in a rather isolated position. However it maintained a steady roll of about 50 children,

Christ Church pupils with Head Mistress,
Mrs. Elizabeth Thorne, c1910.

then aged five to fourteen for girls but only up to the age of about eight for boys who were then transferred to St Mary's. Later on the girls transferred at the age of eleven to the Hungerford Senior School. The teaching complement was Head plus one Assistant, with the help at times of a 'Monitor' (a pupil of about school leaving age).

Life here was uneventful in early days according to the log book, the 'Drill Sergeant', an ex Army chap came regularly to inspect exercises carried out by the children and to set new ones and there was the occasional school outing – one is recorded in 1912 by wagon to Beacon Hill. Strangely there is no reference to the war years of 1914-18 but when it was all over the children were given a 'Peace Mug' and a half day's holiday to go to a 'Peace Tea' at Wallingtons. Diocesan Inspections took place annually to test religious knowledge, followed always by a complimentary report of the visit and a recording of the pupil who had been awarded the 'Bishop's Prize'. In 1915 my mother won it (Was it anything to do with her mother being Headmistress?) and in 1920 it went to Doris Culley (Greenough) and so over the years many present Kintbury people had the honour. The Inspectors always commented on how much they enjoyed their visit to 'this pleasant little school'.

Little is recorded about school activities between the wars but when hostilities broke out again the children's fathers got busy digging an air raid shelter. The school prepared itself to take in evacuees – but none came then – although much later they did. The children helped the war effort by collecting acorns to feed pigs and blackberries for the jam factory. When peace resumed the school continued to operate for about another 18 years though all the time numbers were reducing. This was partly due to smaller families and partly because the new housing in Kintbury was nearer to St. Mary's School. However school life became much more varied. One notable event was taking part in John Schlesinger's film about a local hanging – 'The Black Legend'. Another activity which went on for many years was the making of the school Christmas Cake. This was a 'big' affair. One year the Head Teacher records that it weighed 30lbs and every child in the school had a part in making it. The annual 'baking' took place at the local bakery – no domestic oven being able to cope!

The reputation of Christ Church as a happy and friendly little school continued throughout its life but with a falling roll which was down to 26 in 1962 the time came for it to close and so in January 1963 most children were transferred to St. Mary's with a few going to Inkpen Junior School. The building, with some subsequent additions remains and is now the Bistro Roque Restaurant.

Christ Church Head Teachers	
1900 – 1908	Mrs. Caroline Leonard
1908 – 1922	Mrs. Elizabeth Thorne
1922 – 1948	Miss Hilda Moorby
1948 – 1956	Miss Hilda Whalley
1956 – 1962	Miss Marion Millard

The Misses Clark's School

This was a small private school for young children which operated from the beginning of the century until well after the Second World War. The schoolroom was in the house 'White Lodge' in Newbury Street which in more recent times was the home of the late Dr. and Mrs. Noel Gillman. In the beginning it was run by three sisters and in later years by the two remaining ladies – the Misses Clark. Several local children spent their early years there before transferring to other schools. The sisters were dedicated and kindly ladies still remembered today. Anstace Gladstone (then Goodhart) and Richard Sampson well remember their days at the little school and Anstace tells of riding her pony to school, which was then tethered in Mr. Metcalf's yard nearby whilst lessons were underway.

The Purton Stoke Boys' Preparatory School

This private boarding school originated in Wiltshire where it was attended by Ted Hill of Spinney House and his brothers. The school under its headmaster, Howard Graham-Clark was successful, expanding and needing new premises. At about the same time, in 1944 Ted's father's business, E. Hill & Sons (now Hills of Swindon) bought Barton Court and suggested that the school might like to lease it and so Purton Stoke came to Kintbury, bringing with it employment for quite a number of local people. The school continued to expand and prosper, but in 1963 the headmaster died suddenly and although his wife continued to run it for a few years, falling numbers and other problems caused it to close in 1970. Whilst Mr. Graham-Clark was alive he took an active part in village life, among other things serving on the Parish Council. When the school closed the house was let for a while to the A.T.S. Tyre people but subsequently became a private home again when bought by Sir Terence Conran, whose country house it is today.

Editors note: The section on St. Mary's was submitted by Terry Dillon, Headmaster. Additional log book research and other school items are by Heather Turner.

St. Mary's netball team, late 1930s, outside old school.

The new St. Mary's School (drawing by R. A. Burrow).

Our Farming Community

by Heather Turner

In 1900, within the parish of Kintbury, there were over 20 farm holdings, which shows just how much the village depended upon farming for its trades and employment. Some of these were extremely small, run by the occupier and his family, some were dairy units only and others, usually the larger acreages, combined crop growing with dairying and stock rearing. Most farmers did not own their farms but were tenants of local landowners, particularly the Craven and Sutton estates. Many of these farms no longer exist except in name, usually now attached to the farmhouses, but their past is well remembered – Cullamores, Kiln, Osborne, Osmington, Rooksnest and Sycamore to name a few. About half do remain and are still operating very effectively despite the traumas of the industry today. Among these are Balsdon, Kintbury Farm, Kintbury Holt, Titcombe, Radley and Lord Howard de Walden's extensive holdings at Avington and in the western part of Kintbury.

Farming at the beginning of the century was very labour intensive. There was little mechanisation, restricted mainly to threshing where steam-driven traction engines were used. Ploughs were horse-drawn, milking then was by hand and corn was cut by binders before being stood in stooks by hand to dry. Similarly, hay was made from grass cut by reaper machines, these also horse-drawn. There are stories of some fields being cut by gangs of men scything grass and corn by hand – a practice spilling over from previous centuries. The harvest then was a very special time. A lot had to be done in a short time and when the weather was right, so in addition to their own men many farms took on extra hands, who worked elsewhere during the day – maybe even for another farmer – so they would start at teatime and work until dusk helping to get the harvest in. Their wives and children would follow them into the harvest fields bringing food and drink. Picnics took place with the men snatching a few minutes to eat in between their labours. Their tasks were various, the corn bundles had to be stood in stooks and then when considered dry enough were hand-loaded onto carts and drawn by horse to the ricks in which the corn was stored until the autumn when threshing took place.

Children loved this time because if they behaved themselves they got rides on the empty carts returning to be reloaded. Our picture of a harvest picnic at Irish Hill illustrates the family involvement very well. This was taken in the mid-1920s and things went on with very little change until the Second World War.

John Randall, who farmed at Sycamore Farm in the High Street.

Rick building was a skill passed down from father to son and ricks, hay and corn, were a feature of our local countryside until after the end of the last war. In early years they were thatched to protect against the weather and so kept local thatchers busy. Sometimes ricks stood out in the fields and sometimes the hay and corn were brought to a central place known as a rick yard. One of these, close to the centre of the village, was at Osmington Farm off Wallingtons Road, now a small housing development. This was farmed by Johnny Killick, a resolute man, well known in Kintbury, where he also owned a grocery store, was a parish councillor and much involved in village life. Once his men built a rick across the Titcomb Footpath. This did not please the council who asked him to get it moved. But ricks are not that easy to shift and as I say he was resolute man so the council had to wait until the contents of the rick were needed before the path was clear once again.

After the harvest and before the fields were ploughed in the autumn, 'gleaning' took place. Women and children went to the fields to gather up loose heads of corn to feed their chickens for many families kept hens then for their own supply of eggs. The Second World War was the real turning point in agriculture. Almost overnight, encouraged by the government, tractors took over from the horses. Farm equipment quickly became more and more sophisticated – and expensive! This led to a change for most farmers. They no longer bought many of their own machines but turned to contractors to do many jobs for them and consequently the labour force of earlier years was no longer needed.

As has been mentioned elsewhere, farm workers' wages have been notoriously low throughout this and previous centuries. There were however some compensations. Farmers almost always provided their employees with 'tied' cottages, houses which were usually quite substantially built, especially if they were estate houses. They would be basic by modern standards, but roomy. There was usually an unlimited supply of free firewood, rabbits were plentiful for eating and if it was a dairy farm, free milk was often provided. So, though it was a hard life with long hours, there were some comforts too.

Wartime emphasised the importance of farming. Some workers were called up and some were reserved to work on the land. This left a labour gap which was filled by the recruitment of 'Land Girls'. After training they worked on local farms carrying out a variety of tasks. Hilda Dance, Nora Rose and Sis Braidwood, all living here today, have many tales to tell of the days when they served their country as Land Girls in the Women's Land Army.

When the war ended, changes came about very quickly in the farms close to the centre of the village. Sycamore Farm, which had supplied milk 'by the can' to many people in the High Street area, ceased to exist after the death of John Randall who had farmed there since 1921 and his family since the mid-1800s. John Dopson who farmed at Titcomb and also in the Inkpen Road area, where he kept pigs, sold land for housing, now Bradley Close and Dunn Crescent, and at a later date, that now occupied by The Green and our Nature Reserve. Some lands owned by Killick and Bevan went for housing too. Craven Way, Craven Close, Queens Way, Gainsborough Avenue, Kennet Road and Lawrence Mead now cover a vast area which before the 1940s and 1950s was farmland.

Moving back to Osmington Farm, on John Killick's death this was farmed by his son Peter, for a while, but he decided to sell up and emigrate to Australia so that land was broken up. This left only one farm close to the heart of Kintbury and this was the one previously farmed by Arthur Lawrence of Prospect House. On his death the lands passed to his daughter Winifred and for many years they were leased out, but when Winifred died, Kintbury Farm as it has always been known, passed to another branch of the family and is 'Lawrence' land again, farmed by John Hull.

Moving farther out of the village we are surrounded by agricultural holdings. John Holmes farms at Kintbury Holt, Christchurch and elsewhere; John Freeland at Holt Lodge. Balsdon and Folly Farms are part of a larger complex spilling over into Inkpen; Lindsay Jenkins is at Park Farm off Irish Hill Road and Henry Moore at Elcot and Wawcott has been mentioned in Diane McBride's article. Moving to the west, lands at Hungerford Park, Templeton and Avington farmed before the last war by the Turner family (not related to me), are now part of Lord Howard de Walden's Berkshire estate. On the other side of the A4 are the extensive lands of Radley Farm with its lovely farmhouse which have been farmed for many years by the Gore family. Though I have mentioned most current farmers in this brief summary, some have had to be left out but I have given an indication of how deeply Kintbury is still involved in agriculture even though this is no longer the main provider of employment. The neatness of our hedgerows, our carefully cultivated fields, the healthy livestock seen grazing and the tractor-driven farming equipment moving up and down our lanes and village streets remind us not only of our farming past but our hopes, despite current difficulties, of another century of agricultural prosperity.

Facing page:
The Coles' family in the field at harvest time.

More Farming Memories

by Diane McBride

In 1876, Charles Moore took the train from Chippenham, where he and his family lived and farmed, to Kintbury Station. He walked up to Elcot to look at 500 acres of farmland and then walked to Sutton Estate Office at Benham Valence to meet Sir Richard Sutton and talk about taking over the tenancy of the farm. The deal completed, he walked back to the station to take the train home and organise the move of his family to Elcot, where the Moore family still farm today.

The amount of land farmed by the family has moved up and down over the years. At one time, they farmed land down at Wawcott and stretching as far as Avington, reaching a total of 1200 acres. The farming was mixed, but predominantly good quality dairy short-horns for many years and Charles Moore's son, Frank, went on to win the King George V cup for the best short-horn herd.

At its peak, the Moores employed 21 people. The family were classed as gentleman farmers, not something seen often today, and the farm was essentially run by a foreman, giving the farmer more time for leisure and community activities. Henry remembers that when his grandfather, Frank, needed to move any cattle, he would ride his horse in front of the herd along the road. If the cars didn't stop and give them right of way, Frank wouldn't hesitate to make his position clear by cracking his whip across the windscreen of any driver foolish enough to try and bully Frank and his cattle out of the way. Anyone who dared to challenge Frank would politely be pointed in the direction of Hungerford Police Station to lodge any complaint, with instructions to tell the Police Constable that Frank had sent them! Today, the farm is managed by Henry Moore (Charles Moore's great grandson) plus one herdsman. Contractors are employed to plough and cut for him as needed. This is common practice nowadays as the farmer has the advantage of massive, efficient (not to mention expensive) machinery without having to purchase it and leave it standing idle whilst not in use.

Farming has always been a hard life. Sometimes it seems as if one crisis follows another but they can be a very determined breed and Henry Moore recalls that during the depression in the 1930s, his grandfather, Frank, couldn't find an outlet for their milk. So, he got on the train at Kintbury and travelled, looking for a buyer. When he reached London, he saw a vendor walking along the street with his milk-cart. The sign on the cart read 'Jobs'. The vendor showed him where the Office was and he struck a deal with the owner to supply them with his milk. During the time the farm supplied Jobs, he could identify exactly which street in London was drinking milk from his own cows in Berkshire. The cows were hand-milked until the late 1940s when machinery became more common. Stan Dance, who has lived at Wawcott and worked at Elcot and Wawcott farms all his life, recalls milking the cows as a young boy in the cold winters. When the weather was extremely cold, his hands were kept lovely and warm from the milk but the warmth didn't stop icicles gradually forming on his wrists as he went about the milking.

Some of the people in Kintbury will remember that Wawcott and Elcot were the biggest turkey farmers in the area. During the 1950s, poultry production was at its peak, with around 35,000 turkeys on site at any one time. Stan Dance was in charge of the turkeys and as Harvest finished at the end of September, the run-up to Christmas would start. Turkeys were despatched all over the country to Selfridges, London Hilton, Cruise ships and butchers as far afield as Aldershot, Fleet and Camberley. They were also sold under the name 'Kingfeast Turkeys' from Millets pick-your-own. Smithfield Market was supplied with around 500 birds every week. Henry Moore remembers driving a van full of freshly slaughtered turkeys to Smithfield every night in the weeks before Christmas so the birds would be ready to go on sale the next day. The turkeys really turned the business around and it is due in no small part to this that the Moores were able to continue farming. Today, the only remains of the turkey farming is the Romley Hut which still stands in the farmyard at Wawcott. The hut was bought from the RAF after the War and was used as a (very successful!) brooding house for the turkeys.

Although the turkeys were a very large portion of the business throughout the 1950s, they were not the only part of the business. There were also pigs (around 120 at one time at Elcot), hens and, of course, the dairy herd in addition to the arable land to take care of and, bearing in mind that tractors were still in their relative infancy, only being brought into use in the 1940s, there was still a lot of hard manual labour to be done.

When he was a boy, Stan Dance worked out in the fields all day, ploughing. The horses usually worked in shifts so that no daylight hour was wasted. There were normally three shifts to work. The morning shift would work until mid-day then they would swap with another team which worked until 4 p.m. Then the morning shift would be harnessed up again to work until the daylight went. Unfortunately for the men, the shift system was only applied to the horses so they would be out all day, ploughing up and down with the horses until it was too dark to see. The next day, the team which worked the single shift would do the morning and evening shift and so on. This is how all the work was done, a mix of man and horse power, until the first tractors came along. Orpenham Farm, where Ray Hamblin's family farmed from 1911 to 1986 bought their first tractor in 1941. It was a revelation to them and must have made work a lot easier. Gradually the use of horses dwindled as they were replaced with the new machinery and some of the old carters were taught how to drive the new tractors. It must have been a very different life for them. There was no need to get up at 5 a.m. to feed and water the tractor for a start!

The carters took good care of their horses and brasses and a good example of how much a good horse and their harnesses were worth can be found in an inventory that Henry Moore still has, which was done soon after the Moores moved to Elcot. The list includes 9 horses and harnesses valued at £900, a very high sum of money by anyone's standards in the early part of this century, and 2 horseshoes at £1.10 shillings. Understandably the carters liked to show off their well-groomed horses and brasses at every opportunity and when travelling to Newbury or down to Kintbury station with the cart, they would use only their best, most highly polished harness and brasses. When they travelled any distance, the farmer would allow the carters to take a bundle of straw with them. The carters would sell this along the way to people who kept pigs (most country people kept their own pig to fatten up then) and they would then be allowed to use the money they received for the straw to pay for their beer when they reached town.

The landscape hasn't altered much in this Parish over the last century. Although Stan Dance remembers when the water-meadows, which run alongside Mill Lane, were turned into dry meadows in the last war to make them less labour intensive. Channels were dug out by the Prisoners of War and the river diverted to dry out the meadows. These meadows are still used today for grazing, mostly sheep. Also, at Elcot, most of the hedges were established by Frank Moore who planted them as a thank you to Sir Richard Sutton for his support to the farm during the depression in the 1930s. The demands of today's consumers are shifting and organic or traditional farming is once again more popular, so outdoor pigs and free-range hens are an increasingly common sight in the Berkshire countryside.

Of course we all love our local countryside but many people who today live in the country are forced to travel to work elsewhere. Up until the introduction of tractors, the life of a farmer was a very sociable one and local people not only lived here but worked the land surrounding their homes. Harvest time in particular would see large numbers of people out in the fields, working, eating, drinking and talking together. The warmth and relative comfort of the tractor cab has been traded for the company of others, and although the machines are doubtless more efficient, it must be very isolated compared to the companionable way the work used to be carried out.

Ray Hamblin's family farmed at Orpenham Farm, Winding Wood between 1911 until 1988. His grandfather, William, took over the tenancy in 1911, having previously farmed at Hunts Green Farm, Boxford. The farm was mostly arable, with a small flock of sheep, but between 1945 and 1976 they had a milking herd. Ray's father, Harry Hamblin was one of the first farmers to have their milk collected in bulk by tanker. On 1st February 1955, one of the first milk tankers arrived to make its first collection of seven others from local farms that day. It was more efficient to collect the milk by tanker so to encourage farmers away from churns, Harry was paid an extra farthing a gallon for having his milk collected in bulk.

As with most farms in the area during the war, land girls were employed to help keep the farm going. Ray recalls that the girls used to cycle over from their base in Shefford Woodlands, aptly named some may say, "Lovelocks"!

The farm reverted to total arable farming in 1976 and all 250 acres were devoted to crops until 1988, when Ray's son, Colin, eventually gave up farming.

It seems that whenever we read the newspapers or listen to the news recently, there is more bad news for farmers. Subsidies are of course paid, but they are not as straightforward as a non-farmer may think and even if land is set-a-side, it still has to be managed properly and any time saved by the use of modern machinery is more than taken up by the paperwork demanded by today's legislation. All the farmers and farm workers I spoke to though would not change their lives. Without exception none of them dwelt on the disasters that had befallen them and their families through the century. BSE and foot-and-mouth were never dwelt on during our conversations and those still farming look forward positively to entering the next century doing what they have always done – working the land and feeding not only a hungry nation but an increasingly demanding world market.

A Life in Farming

by Tom Dyer

I've lived in Kintbury a long time, but I was born at Fordingbridge in Hampshire where my father was a farm worker. When I was about to leave school, an uncle who worked in the post office promised he would get me a job there. However, another boy left school a few weeks ahead of me and he got the promised vacancy. I went straight into farming instead – something I've never regretted. My starting wage as a farm boy was seven shillings and sixpence a week (37½ new pence) in 1932. Little did I realise I was to work for my boss, the farmer, Mr. Porter, for the next 44 years.

Farming was a reserved occupation during the war and the nearest I got to battle-dress was my Home Guard uniform. In 1946, the war over, I became engaged to Stella, but we couldn't get married until we had a house and there was none in Fordingbridge. The answer came when Mr Porter decided to buy Hamstead Holt Farm on the Craven estate 'lock, stock and barrel'. This meant that the farmer acquired the tenancy of the farm and took over the farm stock, equipment and responsibility for the existing employees at an agreed valuation from the outgoing tenant. There was a spare cottage and I was offered employment as cowman with the cottage if I would move from Fordingbridge. A cottage! Of course I gladly accepted and Stella and I were married in October 1946.

Hamstead Holt was a farm of 300 acres with a herd of 50/60 cows, for which I had full responsibility. My wages were then just over £2 a week, but I was able to work overtime which added another pound and a bit, and we had a rent-free cottage and free milk. The cottage was pretty basic, even for that time, the immediate post World War II period. There was no mains water or sanitation – water came from a spring; there was an outside closet, lamps used paraffin, our old and inefficient kitchen range burnt wood or coal, and there was a strange tin oven fuelled with paraffin. Stella was a London girl and it took her a little while to get used to these bare necessities. Like most rural housing there was a large garden and we had plenty of farm manure. With this combination I grew the vegetables which tasted good, and won some prizes at the Horticultural shows over the years.

We'll never forget our first winter in Kintbury, it was so cold; everything was rationed and we'd had no opportunity to build up a reasonable coal stock over the summer months before we moved in. Stella remembers we put everything on the bed, including my old Home Guard overcoat, but we woke early covered in frost. When we visited Stella's old home at Christmas, my mother-in-law packed a large suitcase of coal for me to take home. Lugging it back to Kintbury, I found the coalman had just been!

Those post-war years signalled a small revolution in farming practice due to improvements in mechanisation. At Hamstead Holt milking was by machine, instead of by hand. The horses had gone and the carter became the tractor driver. But the days of the combine harvester had still to come, and harvest-time brought part-time help from men in the village who worked in very different trades. The blacksmith came, the postman, men who worked in Hungerford and Newbury factories – all were 'strappers' who turned up at the farm to work an extra turn when their regular day's work was over.

The beginning of mechanisation.
An early tractor alongside a farm cart in late 1940s.

In the early days a Hamstead Holt the milk no longer went to the railway station, but was picked up in large heavy steel churns by road lorry. As time passed, the churns were made of aluminium alloy and became lighter. Then came the milk tanker and further improvements in the milking process, so that one man could now handle more than twice as many cows for milking.

There was a shortage of labour in the post-war days and my one day off each week often went by the board, and several years I went without an annual holiday. There were compensations, I liked my boss and I've always enjoyed the beauty of nature around me. The sky always seemed to be full of sky-larks then. Pee-wits nested in the fields, and when we went over with the harrow in the spring, if we spotted a nest, we'd pick it up with bird and eggs still intact and put it in the hedge.

In 1952 electricity came to our cottage and we enjoyed the unbelievable luxury of electric light. At that time we had a small windfall and in 1956 acquired one of the first television sets in the village, though we still had a radio powered by accumulator, a type of electric cell battery which we had to take to a local shop to get re-charged. As the years went by our cottage suffered from lack of maintenance and in 1974 Stella and I were offered one of the council houses in Laylands Green, built in 1938 to replace the notoriously bad cottages in what was then called Pig Lane.

In 1976 a change of government policy gave farmers financial inducement to give up dairy farming and concentrate on beef production. Our milking herd was sold and my job came to an end. Having been continuously employed on the farm from 1936 to 1980, the changes that came in milking methods seemed to creep up on one, but looking back from 1936 to now, the changes are truly dramatic. One has to admit that a lot of the 'sweat' has been eliminated, but also the numbers employed have dropped tremendously. Another downside to the arrival of the combine was the taking out of hedges to make larger fields, to enable the large combines to work efficiently. It was this, together with the coming of silage making that has so reduced the numbers of field-nesting birds. Sky-larks still linger on in a few places, likewise the lap-wings, but very little stubble is left unploughed over the winter, so removing the food for seed-eating small birds and partridges. Set-aside, a scheme whereby farmers can claim a payment to leave a percentage of their land unploughed and uncropped to reduce the so-called corn mountains has helped considerably, but one cannot visualise this continuing for ever.

During my 24 years at Laylands Green, some building plans were submitted for the adjacent field, very boggy, with a spread of numerous ponds, the home of a very established colony of great crested newts. This building development was opposed as it would spell the end of the newts and eventually this opposition was successful and Kintbury now has its own aptly named 'Kintbury Newt Ponds Reserve' ably managed by B.B.O.N.T.

We've talked about the birds and machinery changes, so let's give a mention to all of us who lived through those years of change. There were an awful lot of employed men all living in tied cottages or in villages close to their work. We all knew each other well and visited our 'local' for a pint and a game of darts, crib, shove ha'penny or dominoes. Naturally when problems arose in our working conditions, we discussed them, and we all agreed that the Farmworkers' Union was the obvious body to assist and guide us. So it soon came about that every village had its own union branch. However, with the care of animals involved, it was obvious that strike action was out, so our

Opening the Newt Ponds Reserve 1998.
The author is on the left.

problems or demands had to be negotiated. However, without the big stick of strike action, farmworkers wages have always been the lowest of any industry. Apart from the serious side of union activity a real social feeling developed among members, and darts matches between branches created loads of enjoyment, including our wives as well. Nowadays with so few full-time farmworkers, these small village branches have disappeared and with it has gone much happy fellowship. However, Kintbury has numerous organisations to suit all tastes. The Horticultural Society is thriving, there are sports clubs for young and old. A Wildlife Group started 12 years ago has grown from seven members to one hundred now. Another success story, to my mind, is the Kintbury Volunteer Group doing a fantastic job helping our community in numerous ways. These jottings paint a sort of picture of the 20th century; I wonder what the next century has in store for us all.

Industries and Occupations

by Heather Turner and Sybil Flinn

Many changes have taken place in Kintbury's industries and occupations during this century. In 1900 most activities related to farming and meeting the needs of the village, or were based on the use of local natural resources – in other words, Clay, Chalk and Gravel.

The presence of suitable clay deposits meant that Kintbury already had a thriving Brickmaking business, dating before the beginning of this century and supplying mostly local needs because of the difficulty of transporting such heavy materials. In 1900 the brickworks were run by George Thomas Killick, and both bricks and tiles were made. Bricks were hand made in moulds bearing the initials of 'G.T.K. Kintbury'. Samples can still be found today when rebuilding or demolition work is being done. The Brickworks were in Laylands Green (then Pig Lane) at Kiln Green. Clay was dug from pits in the Barrymores, Blandys Hill and Laylands Green areas and transported by horse and cart to the brickyard where it was worked and moulded into bricks. These were then placed in open sheds to dry out before being 'fired' in one of the two kilns. Tiles were also made. For many years there was an interesting product of the firing operation – local people brought potatoes to bake in the cooling ashes of the kilns.

Brickmaking continued well into the 1920s. By then the Killick family, whose daughter had met and married a soldier called Eli Bevan, who had been convalescing at Barton Court during the First World War, were becoming more interested in dairy farming. A partnership was formed – Killick & Bevan – and a milk delivery service started up, delivering by horse and trap around the Kintbury area, and this was to continue for many years. Later a niece of the Bevans, Carrie Evans, came to help in the dairy and on the round and is well remembered as she lived here for many years and still resides in Newbury. Later still, Elsie Turfrey was employed and tells her own story in this book. However, the brickmaking came to an end, superseded by mass manufacture and easy transportation in the 20s.

Another industry, dating back to earlier times, was Whiting Manufacture. Chalk was excavated and the product, Whiting, was used for all sorts of purposes – in the making of paint, colour washes, talcum powder and various domestic products, depending on the quality and texture of the chalk. The first Whiting works had been behind Kintbury Mill, where Millbank is now, and here there was massive excavation of chalk, bringing about the escarpment now known as The Cliffs. However, by 1900 this business had ceased operating. A second works was operating earlier this century in the Irish Hill area, the canal being used to transport products to the railway yard for loading on to rail wagons. The Irish Hill chalk was not of high quality and this probably had something to do with the demise of the business after a fairly short time through becoming unprofitable. The machinery remained in-situ for many years and some is still there but totally hidden by trees and undergrowth. A photograph survives of the pugmill, used for grinding up the chalk and one of the relics still at Irish Hill.

The third works was in Inkpen Road, Kintbury, now the site of Great Severals. This was in operation until the 1940s. The owner, who will be remembered by some, was Frederick Tuttle, a significant figure, rarely seen without his Airedale dog, and shown in the photograph below.

Chalk was dug for his works from Newbury Street, Burtons Hill and Inkpen Road areas, the latter being cut from tunnels as opposed to the open-cast cutting from other pits. Chalk blocks were conveyed from the other pits to Inkpen Road and normally four men were employed in the cutting and manufacturing work. Freddy himself did not get too involved in the daily activities but 'supervised' in a rather gentlemanly fashion. His wife was also much involved in the business – particularly keeping a close eye on all money matters! Here also chalk was ground in a pugmill operated with a mule. Local people remember as children being sent down to the Whiting Works for a 'knob of chalk' costing two pence (old money) and used for whitening doorsteps and other purposes in the home.

Gravel was dug from local pits well before 1900 and continued through this century spasmodically right up to the 70s. In the early days there was a constant demand for gravel to keep the roads and footpaths under repair. Because of the difficulty of transporting this heavy material before motorised vehicles, it tended to be dug from pits nearest to the required use. It had to be dug by hand, then loaded onto carts and drawn by horses. Pits in use in the early days were at Irish Hill, Blandys Hill and Barton Court. The first two pits closed early on but the Barton Court pit continued until sometime in the 30s when it was closed for many years. Coming to more recent times, in the 50s sand and a coarser aggregate, produced by crushing the pebbles which abound in the Christ Church area, were dug from land opposite Christ Church School (now the Bistro Roque). This did not last long as the process proved difficult and too labour intensive to be a profitable venture.

However, down at Barton Court, by then owned by Hills of Swindon, the old gravel workings took on a new lease of life in the 1970s with the building of the M4 motorway. Though only a shallow bed it was extensively worked with modern equipment to provide aggregate for the road and then reinstated as farm land. All that remains today is a small service area, used by Hills and a transfer for onwards transmission to other locations as filling material.

All the foregoing activities provided employment for relatively small numbers of men. Another early activity was at the 'Old Laundry' as it is known today. This no longer exists but was located on the present site of the terrace of three houses, 53-57 High Street, which are actually built on the foundations of the demolished laundry. The laundry was originally built as public baths (see the article on the Dunn family). This probably accounts for the fact that it looks more like a chapel than a laundry, a popular architectural style in the late nineteenth century.

Workers setting off for an outing from the old Laundry in High Street.

A number of young women were employed, with the intention of providing them with training and useful employment. Older women also helped out when the laundry was particularly busy. From 1900 it was supervised in turn by two ladies, the latter being Mrs Gilbert, who lived next door at Combe View, part of which was used as a hostel for some of the girls employed. Mrs. Gilbert was a very practical lady, well respected and very orderly with her washing lines. She was particular, for instance, that the underpants of eminent local gentlemen should not be pegged up next to the drawers of respectable local spinsters! It has not been possible to establish exactly when the laundry closed, but it was finally demolished around 1922 and houses built in its place, these being first occupied in 1925.

Just over the parish boundary with Inkpen were the Inkpen Sawmills between Post Office and Folly Roads. Though not in Kintbury this business, with origins going back into the nineteenth century, had close connections with Kintbury. It was run by the Edwards' family, who at one time had land holdings in Kintbury. Items such as farm and domestic gates, fencing, wheelbarrows and coffin boards were made. Some wood used came from elsewhere and would have been brought in by rail, possibly by canal and later by road. In the First World War much of its production turned to the making of ammunition boxes and many women were employed. The Edwards owned tracts of local woodland for felling purposes. Cutting and hauling of timber was an important part of their business, some of which would have been used in the furniture trade and some for props for shoring purposes. In early times, all the hauling was done by horses and timber wagons, then by steam and later by diesel driven tractors and equipment. For many years after mechanical transport arrived, some horses were kept on for the purposes of hauling out of difficult wooded areas, a practice which is now being reintroduced in other parts of the country.

The heyday of the saw mills was undoubtedly the between-the-wars' period, when their products had a well-deserved reputation for quality. After the Second World War, with members of the Edwards' family growing older and diversifying into other interests, the business declined, was eventually sold and after a while closed down. The site was divided up, with industrial units built on part – the idea being to provide employment for local people – and the rest became a small housing development, so it is difficult to imagine what it was like in its prime. Employment was provided for many local men and women. One of the Kintbury women was Gertrude Holmes – 'Gert' as she was known to everyone. She was there for most of her working life and she operated a small

circular saw from which other employees kept a very respectable distance, but which Gert handled with ease and never got as much as a scratch. She was a hard working lady – and tough. Everyday and in all weathers, she walked from her home to the mills by the shortest route, which was the Titcomb footpath.

Other businesses operating between 1900 and about 1950 were very much related to the land and its needs. There were forges at Elcot (still going strong) and also in Station Road (now Forge Cottage), the High Street and in the Square. These dealt with the shoeing of horses and plied the blacksmith's trade producing and repairing ironmongery for farmers and other local people. Mr Waite, who operated on the former garage site in the Square, was a Wheelwright, another necessary trade of former times. All this was to be replaced with the coming of the motor car by our first garage employing mechanics – as cars and other vehicles replaced the horse.

Kintbury had a garage serving local needs almost continuously since the 1920s. This former business, so much a part of Kintbury and in the Square, was operated for many years by the Druce family, who took over from Mr. Burridge shortly after the Second World War Laurie (Lawrence) Druce and his wife Ethel, were both very much involved in the business as they were in village life. Laurie sadly died quite a few years ago but Ethel, now 90, is a regular member of local clubs and still lives in Bendor House, part of which was the garage office, where many small gatherings took place and customers could be sure of being updated on local happenings. Their son, Michael, took over the business for a while but eventually it was sold and soon after closed down to be replaced by the present housing development of Kintbury Square and new terraced cottages on Station Road. Meanwhile, a new garage opened up sometime after the Second World War in Newbury Street, on the site of a former whiting working.

Another well-remembered business was that of the Watercress Beds, just out of the village on the Hungerford road. This was owned by Mr. Wootton, who lived at 49 High Street, and was a member of the Wootton family at Ramsbury who grew watercress there on a rather larger scale. However, the Kintbury person who will always be associated with the Kintbury beds was Dick Mills. The beds, with their water channels were immaculately cultivated, and every day in the growing season the cress was cut, bunched, packed in wickerbaskets and taken by punt along the canal to Kintbury Station, to be dispatched by passenger train in the late afternoon to London. Dick was usually assisted in this task by various local schoolboys, the rewards being a ride back up the canal on the punt. The business operated during the 20s and 30s and after the Second World War, but disappeared some years ago when cress was grown elsewhere on a much larger commercial scale and hygienically sealed in plastic bags – not the same at all!

Up to the Second World War, employment for a large percentage of Kintbury men was on local farms, which were very labour intensive. In the post-war years modern farming methods and mechanisation has reduced the labour force needed, many times over, and so employment is sought elsewhere and largely outside the village area.

For women early this century employment was also very different. Most, on leaving school found themselves 'in service', that is as live-in or daily maids. This was a hard life, extremely poorly paid, but providing accommodation if you lived in (no mean consideration if you came from a large family in a small house) and often very good food. This account by a Kintbury lady of 'life in service' says it all!

'I was one of sixteen staff. I started at 16 as Scullery Maid at Denford House (now Norland Nursery Training College). My job was preparing the vegetables, washing up and scrubbing tables and floors. We started at 5.45 am and were lucky to get to bed by 11 o'clock. We had half a day off each week and every other Sunday from three o'clock to nine. We slept three to a bedroom most of the time. We were paid £1.00 per month (£12.00 a year). We had very good food and were quite happy but things were tough in those days. We had to go into the Dining Room for prayers at 9 o'clock each morning and to church each Sunday morning one week and afternoons the next. If we were not there, we were in trouble on Monday morning at prayers and lost one hour of our next day off. I stayed for a year and then went to London as a Kitchen Maid. My pay doubled – ten shillings (50p) a week. Very wealthy!'

Usually before World War 2, when women married and started a family they gave up work. It seemed easier to live (?exist) on one wage then. Besides running a house with no labour-saving devices, cooking for the family and rearing the children was a full-time job on its own. The outbreak of war in 1939 brought an end to this: women were needed for war work, often in jobs previously done by men. They became accustomed to working and looking after the home, and then it became a necessity to maintain a reasonable standard of living. House-owning and high rents had a lot to do with this. Neither of these factors applied before the war in Kintbury. Besides which, many more career opportunities were available in later years.

So we come to the present day and here the most significant development has been the setting up of Sir Terence Conran's Company 'Benchmark', at Barton Court. Set up some 16 years ago by Conran, furniture maker Sean Sutcliffe, and Wendy Jones, Benchmark's original purpose was to design and make prototype pieces of furniture and shop-fittings for Storehouse, the conglomerate comprising of Mothercare, Habitat, BHS, the Conran Shop, Heals and other companies.

Benchmark's design studio and manufacturing premises are accommodated in the old stables and estate buildings of Barton Court. Traffic is routed directly from the A4 and consequently many local people are unaware of Benchmark's existence! In 1998, an old farm barn situated on adjoining land, was extensively renovated to create a new 14,000 sq.ft. factory. Another old building, still known as the 'calf shed' is currently being converted to a show-room.

From the beginning, Benchmark has sought to recruit and train young local people to staff the business. The total work-force now numbers 30, making the company the largest employer in Kintbury, and each year pupils from local schools are given the opportunity to take their work experience period at Benchmark. Every summer, two or three school leavers are offered a 3-year apprenticeship in furniture making. Two of Benchmark's early apprentices are now in key management positions.

Benchmark today is regarded as being at the forefront of British furniture design and manufacture and its output is sold in Conran shops in London, Paris and Hamburg, soon to be joined by two new shops in New York and Paris and through franchise stores in Japan. The company also manufactures fittings and furniture for all the Conran restaurants as well as working for many internationally renowned architects. Some 70% of the goods manufactured by Benchmark are exported.

Maybe rural artisanship is no longer in agricultural employment, but Benchmark's example shows that local communities can benefit from good training, good jobs and well-converted agricultural buildings. It is also an interesting thought that the customers at the very fashionable Conran restaurants in London and Paris are sitting on chairs and at tables designed and made in Kintbury.

Today employment for local people is also provided at Inglewood Health Hydro, the Jarvis Hotel at Elcot Park, the Bistro Roque and other small local businesses. Present-day Kintbury folk are extremely enterprising and so many are self employed in activities too numerous to list, and ranging from the artistically creative, e.g. Interior Design and Pottery, to the burgeoning world of I.T. In another one hundred years, which of our new industries will be regarded with the same quaintness as Brickmaking and Whiting manufacture are today?

Above: Cutting and loading timber at Kintbury Wharf, now the Dundas Arms car park.

Below left: Blocks of whiting stored in shed at Tuttle's works in Inkpen Road, now Great Severals.

Below: Interior of part of Benchmark's workshops at Barton Court.

Forging Ahead into the Next Century

by Diane McBride

Geoffrey Sampson, the Blacksmith at Elcot, can trace his family back over several generations and watching him work is like stepping back in time. His family have worked here in the same Forge for over 350 years. It is probably one of the few rural professions where little has changed in the last century and this business has been passed from father to son for generations. Together with his sons Robert and Phillip they look after clients within about half-hour distance of Newbury. In fact, one of the few changes to their way of working is that they now travel to the horses rather than the other way around. Geoffrey makes the shoes in his forge at Elcot ready for his sons to collect and take out on their rounds. In his father's and grandfather's day, their customers would just turn up at The Forge, often having travelled distances of up to 3 miles, and wait in-line for their horses to be shod. These days, appointments are made well in advance and the Blacksmith goes to them so the horses do not have to travel far from their own stable doors! The Sampsons are all Blacksmiths (the difference between a Farrier and a Blacksmith is that a Farrier shoes horses, a Blacksmith shoes horses and in addition is a qualified iron worker) and Geoffrey is currently the most highly qualified Blacksmith in the district. In former days, the blacksmith was the motor mechanic and metal worker of the time making everything from needles to plough shares. In his spare time he still creates pieces of ornamental ironwork, many of them commissioned, such as the front for the Newbury Methodist Church.

In 1970 he was granted the Freedom of the City of London for his expertise in taking care of Her Majesty's treasured racehorses. He received his Royal Warrant in 1974, as did his father in 1966, for shoeing the Queen's racehorses at Polehampton Stud, Kingsclere. His skills are much sought after and in 1986 he judged the Best Shod Horse at the Horse of the Year Show. His list of four-legged clients reads like an Equine VIP list. They include 'English Prince', winner of the 1974 Irish Derby and 'Imperial Prince' who came in second, 'Queen's Hussar' at Highclere stud and 'Brigadier Gerard', trained by Major Dick Hern. Despite these famous 'clients', Geoffrey and his sons treat all horses with the same kind, firm manner, no matter how much they are worth or who they belong to. There are many examples of the skill and patience this family applies to their work but there is one in particular which you can

Geoffrey Sampson in his forge at Elcot.

sense gives Geoffrey a quiet sense of satisfaction. There is a photograph on the wall in the forge of a client and her horse, who had been lame for many years. She brought her horse to Geoffrey to see if he could help. He made the horse special built-up shoes which corrected his lameness and they went on to claim first prize in a veterans class – the horse was 33 at the time.

Geoffrey's younger son, Phillip, now lives with his family in the house next to the Forge at Elcot which has recently been built to replace the old house where his own Great Grandfather, William Sampson lived. Hopefully there will still be a Sampson living and working in the same place in another 350 years.

There are currently over 2,000 registered farriers nationwide. Years ago, of course, their work included shoeing the shires used in farming and the ponies used to pull the carts and traps which were used as main transport. Today, the work is predominantly looking after the feet of horses used for more leisurely pursuits, albeit that some of them are celebrities themselves in the racing world, but it is reassuring to know that, in at least one area of rural life machinery will never be able to replace this type of craftsmanship and skill.

Kintbury Mill

by Sybil Flinn

There can be no building in Kintbury which has seen so many diverse changes in the 20th century as Kintbury Mill. Kintbury's entry in the Domesday Book of 1086 records three mills, and the building we see today is the successor of much earlier buildings. The present structure dates from the late 18th century and was already standing when the canal was constructed.

At the beginning of this century the mill was owned by Mr. Henry Phillips. Besides the building, there seem to have been a number of smaller single-storey sheds on the same site. The 1891 census records a Saddler/Harness maker on the site, and we believe that one of these buildings used to be a Silk Mill earlier in the 19th century. By 1912 Mr. Henry Phillips had died or retired and his son, Harold Edgar Phillips was the miller. Harold Phillips was also quite an entrepreneur. In 1912 he was both miller and coal merchant, and he also ran an electricity plant at the mill powered by a water-driven dynamo. Our photograph shows the plant building at the rear of the mill, and the foundations and inlet ducts for the water can still be seen today. This was the first electricity to be available in Kintbury and among customers supplied were the shops in Church Street and some private homes, such as Osmington House.

Harold Phillips also built houses, examples being The Cliffs and Harold Road, and he lived in the large house now named Millers House in Station Road, which overlooked the mill. Mr. Phillips was also the owner of Park Farm.

In 1940 the mill was acquired by the Feathery Flake Co. of Bristol and was converted into a flour-packing plant. Mrs. Lillian Bentley recalls this stage of the mill's life very clearly. Lill had come to Kintbury as an evacuee from London with her mother, living with her mother's brother in the Crescent. Lill was widowed when her husband of barely a month was killed at Dunkirk, and although she was later to remarry, to Harry Bentley in 1943, at this stage she wanted to find work. Answering an advertisement for staff, Lill was taken on and later, when the foreman retired, Lill became forewoman of the mill.

Flour arrived at the mill in bulk from Bristol. At Kintbury the flour was mixed in various blends and packed in bags for sale to the public. About 20 women and girls worked at the mill, as well as drivers of the delivery lorries and support staff. The mill was a busy place and its output overtook that of its Bristol plant. Kintbury mill continued in Feathery Flake's ownership until 1960 when it closed its operations and the buildings were put up for sale. Eventually the mill was sold and with a little interior conversion, the ground floor became The Old Mill Restaurant. Then the upper floor was turned into a night club called 'Kinters'.

The old building made an attractive place for its new use: the bar was over the mill-race and a glass floor was fitted in this area so that customers could see the water flowing by as they supped their drinks. The enterprise although popular with the customers was not so in the neighbourhood; parked cars became a problem and late-night noise a general nuisance. The business was eventually forced to close and the buildings put up for sale again.

For some time the mill stood empty but was then acquired by Trencherwood for housing development. Complete refurbishment of the site resulted in the development as seen today. The main mill building was converted into five flats and the old industrial buildings along the waterside were demolished and five terraced cottages built in their place. At the rear another smaller new building contained four more flats. Care was taken to retain as many features of the old property as possible. The small cottage at the end of the mill which Harry and Lill Bentley had lived in for some years remained, and so did the roof beams in the top-most flats, and the glass floor over the water is a talking point in the living room of the ground-floor flat.

In 1985 the National House Building Council made Trencherwood an Award for Achievement in Housing Design – well deserved: Kintbury Mill is a most attractive place to live.

'Feathery Flake' workers outside the mill during war-time. Charlie Poole the foreman in centre, Lil Bentley on his left, Jack Hibberd on right and Bernice Hibberd fourth on left. Can you identify others?

The Mills, Kintbury.

Kintbury Mill in 1900 – and in 1999.

Getting There

by Heather Turner

In Kintbury in 1900 there were no buses, and no local car ownership is recorded. But we did have the railway which provided a regular passenger and goods service. Originally it was the Berks and Hants line and a station was opened here as far back as 1847. But by the beginning of the century the Great Western Railway had taken over the line which gave them, as now, easy access to London as well as serving the local area. The station was well equipped with staff, buildings and goods sidings. Railway staff were held in some respect then and the Stationmaster himself was of some local importance and standing in his distinctive G.W.R. uniform. His house adjoined the station with its own access to the platform so he could keep an eye on things at all times. His platform staff consisted of two porters who were capable and versatile men.

The 'Up' platform boasted some rather nice and typical railway buildings painted in the G.W.R. livery of chocolate and cream. These consisted of a general waiting room, another smaller room for ladies only, male and female lavatories and of course the Stationmaster's office which also served as the booking office. On cold winter days, fires would be lit in all rooms but the one that burned brightest was in the Stationmaster's office! Here the 'gentry' would be invited in or invite themselves, to wait for their 'London train'. Regular travellers in early days were Lord Burnham from Barton Court, the Walmesleys from Inglewood, the Gladstones from Wallingtons and the Turners from Hungerford Park, the latter preferring Kintbury to Hungerford station. Later, another regular daily commuter to London was Mr. Goodhart of New Mill.

What a pity all the station platform buildings were demolished in 1978 in a railway rationalisation exercise. Until well past the middle of the century there was considerable goods traffic activity. Timber was despatched, cattle came and went. Coal arrived and was distributed by local hauliers. Milk in churns, watercress and the Royal Mail were taken daily to the station for onward conveyance by passenger train, but by the late 1950's all these activities were declining and eventually disappeared altogether as road transport took over. Gone forever are the goods trains that roared through the night, steam driven and counted rather than sheep by those of us enduring a sleepless night! Keith Gilbert's interesting article gives a much more detailed account of railway activity at Kintbury.

But in the early days there was a great spirit of pride and comradeship among the local railway staff – 'God's Wonderful Railway' remember! The photograph of the 'Railway Supper' held at the Red Lion (Dundas Arms) in 1912 illustrates this well.

Ordinary people also made good use of the railway, though in the early days this was likely to be infrequently, maybe for a visit to Newbury on Market Day or to travel farther afield. Cost would have been one factor and there was less need as the village was very much self-contained with a variety of shops and employment available locally. As the century progressed this changed and by the late 1930s many more used trains to travel to work, school and to shop. Travel reached its peak between 1940 and 1960 after which there was a considerable decline with many

Staff of Kintbury Station with invited guests at their Railway Supper, 1912, held at the Dundas Arms.

The Giles' carrier van with members of the family, which served Hungerford, Kintbury and Marsh Benham.

turning to the use of cars instead. Early days saw other forms of transport used for people and goods. Horses and carts conveyed virtually all materials locally, though there was some use of the canal, which is referred to in another chapter. In 1900 the Red Lion (Dundas Arms) was still advertising 'Post Horses and Carriages' for hire.

People also travelled by pony and trap – if they could afford to! Some rode horses and at least two houses in Kintbury still have tethering rings. Many had bicycles and their use increased as time went by. Otherwise 'getting there' meant walking, with local footpaths used out of necessity and not just for exercise and pleasure. Those linking the village with places like Avington, Elcot, Titcomb and Inkpen (many worked at the Sawmills there) had to be kept under constant repair, then a responsibility of the Parish Council.

By the 1920s young people leaving school and finding work in Newbury frequently cycled to and fro in all weathers and in the dark in winter. Bicycle lighting was poor and provided by smelly acetylene lamps before the coming of batteries and dynamos.

Soon after the Second World War started, by which time cars were in rather more use, the government directed they were to be 'laid up' for the duration due to strict petrol rationing. Only essential vehicles were allowed so more use was made of bicycles. It was then that the strange contraption used by my mother made its reappearance. This was a 'bicycle and sidecar', the latter shaped rather like an old-fashioned pram and attached to the bike like a motorcycle and sidecar. This conveyed my younger brother and sister, then aged about two and four, sitting one behind the other. I well remember one particular occasion when we were riding through Denford

and approaching Dunn Mill. We were in convoy; father first, then mother with kids, then my older brother and me bringing up the rear on our little bikes. There was a gate then by the bridge and a kind lady opened it for us. On went father, mother with kids and my brother. Then the lady caught sight of the sidecar and was so fascinated she let the gate go and it swung back, hit my bike and shot me and it into the River Dunn!

After the First World War transport by road underwent a really big change and motorised vehicles capable of carrying lots of people and goods of all descriptions began to appear. Some of these were ex-army lorry chassis adapted to commercial use and others were newly manufactured, based on wartime expertise. The operators were often local people around the Newbury area who had previously had 'Carrier' businesses using horses and cars. So, by the early 1920s, open-topped charabancs were available for excursions to local beauty spots and events. Then came covered buses and these were used to establish the first local scheduled services, mainly with Newbury as the destination. Again, these were run by enterprising local people. Albert Greenwood, who lived at 2 Newbury Street, ran a service from Kintbury in partnership with John Burt from Inkpen, until in the early 1930s they, with many others, were amalgamated into the newly formed Newbury and District Motor Services. Albert continued to work for this company and also became a booking agent for excursions from Kintbury by coach. About the same time as bus services were being set up, motorised Carrier Services started. A Mr. Beavis of 7 Station Road, where he had a small shop, was one carrier. Others serving Kintbury were Mr. Percy Giles of Hungerford and also Mr. George Giles of Kintbury (these two not related). People would ask them to fetch everything from groceries to clothing and furniture from shops in Newbury, for which they would charge a small commission. Often items were brought back 'on approval' – even intimate things like corsets and ladies' fleecy knickers, from emporiums such as Beynons, Dexter Robinsons and Inch's – all long gone.

'Outings' featured throughout the century. Early ones were by horse and cart hired from local farmers and by traction engine and trailer. For obvious reasons they did not go far – Combe and Beacon Hills were favourites. Charabancs ventured farther. For example, by 1920 excursions from Newbury were being advertised to Southsea, London, Henley Regatta and Ascot Races. Those early vehicles, being open-topped, were only used in summer, the bodies removed from the chassis and replaced by van-type tops and used for haulage work in the winter. By the late 1920s canvas hoods were attached to the excursion vehicles and the summer tripping business grew with Kintbury featuring as a regular picking-up point. One well-remembered outing organised from Kintbury happened round about 1935 when the church and chapels got together and arranged a huge excursion needing several coaches for all their Sunday School children. I don't think this has been done since. The Great Western Railway also ran 'Specials'. Ted Hall remembers one trip to Tidworth Tattoo for only 2/6d (12 1/2 p) including entrance money – very good value he thought. Trips to Pewsey Carnival ran every year until comparatively recently, and Kintbury Football Club used to 'charter' trains for away matches.

Coach trips continue to be popular today with many of our local clubs having 'away days' to different places and at some distance, made possible by our motorway network.

It was not until well after the Second World War that car ownership gradually became affordable to many more people and with this – or probably partially because of it – there was a serious decline in the availability of public transport. Cars then became a necessity for many people to get to work and a convenience for taking children to school as well as shopping. Not only that, the ease of this form of travel and a very considerable increase in the number of houses built in Kintbury, brought us a sizeable 'commuting' population working in London, Reading, Basingstoke, Swindon and many other places some distance away. Gone too were the earlier opportunities of employment in the village which marked the beginning of the century. Will this change I wonder, as we progress beyond 2000, with significant numbers working from home at the end of a computer terminal? Young people too insist on the independence of having their own four wheels for college, work and social activities, so it is not unusual for us to have four- and five-car families, leading to congestion on residential roads and particularly on our narrow streets. What to do about this occupies residents, shopkeepers and the Parish Council today. Do we restrict parking with double yellow lines and how do we 'calm' traffic as we reach the end of the century? Volume of vehicles and lack of public money brings us another problem as our roads fall into even greater disrepair, something which curiously also occupied our Parish Council in the year 1900. Maybe we really will have to abandon the car for the bicycle as we are urged to do, and for which we are being encouraged by the current initiative to make our canal towpath into part of a National Cycleway.

Early outing to the seaside.

Kintbury and its Railway

by Keith Gilbert

On 21st December 1847 the Berks and Hants Railway opened for business with Kintbury Station being the last before Hungerford on the new Branch line from Reading. It had one other line from Reading to Basingstoke. By 1900 the Hungerford line was absorbed into the Great Western Railway and the line had been extended on to Great Bedwyn and farther into the West Country. The idea was to develop a shorter route to Exeter, Plymouth and Penzance so that the GWR could better compete with its rival – the London and South Western Railway (LSWR) whose route was then much shorter causing the GWR route via Swindon, Bristol and Taunton to be nicknamed the 'Great Way Round'. The new route was completed in 1906 and from that day to the present Kintbury has seen the Cornish Riviera and Torbay Expresses with others roaring through on their way south-westwards. Soon the LSWR was unable to compete and the GWR developed a massive holiday traffic. Local traffic also increased and in 1910 an extra siding was installed at Kintbury to cope with the volume of goods being carried by rail.

The arrangements at Kintbury for the handling of freight traffic were quite simple. The sketch map shows these arrangements. The sidings had an 'end loading dock' for vehicles, these would have been for horse drawn vehicles originally and would have been pushed onto the railway wagons by hand after the horses had been unharnessed. Later motor vehicles could have been accepted. There was a cattle loading dock which enabled the cattle to be driven up a ramp to the level of the cattle 'box' so that they could enter the wagon through side doors. A five ton capacity crane was permanently installed at a fixed location so that heavy items could be unloaded from wagons onto horse drawn carts etc. or vice-versa.

Baskets of watercress and other goods awaiting the London train (c.1920).

This machine was hand powered by two huge handles, rather like an enormous Meccano crane that kids could build from their Meccano sets. There was a goods shed that enabled wagons and vans to be unloaded under cover and the goods stored rather like a miniature warehouse. This structure was quite big and could house three railway wagons. There was a raised platform inside for level access to the wagons and on the other side there were further doors so that carts could be 'backed up' and loaded direct from the wagons across the platform. Another small fixed crane was inside the shed hand-driven for lifting heavy boxes etc. Finally outside the level of the ground was raised up to the top of the rails in some areas to enable coal lorries to be loaded direct from the coal wagons. Given the era when these facilities were in use they were quite well thought out and minimised the amount of manual effort required, but even with this consideration the amount of physical manhandling of freight was enormous.

Milk in churns from local farms, watercress and other perishable goods were handled via the passenger station. However, during the inter-war period road transport was already eating into railway freight traffic, with something of a revival occurring during World War Two. As a kid I can remember the goods yard being full of wagons bringing in supplies for the nearby American army camps – sometimes in excess of 50 trucks.

When the war ended Kintbury reverted to a sleepy backwater. Road hauliers continued to take more and

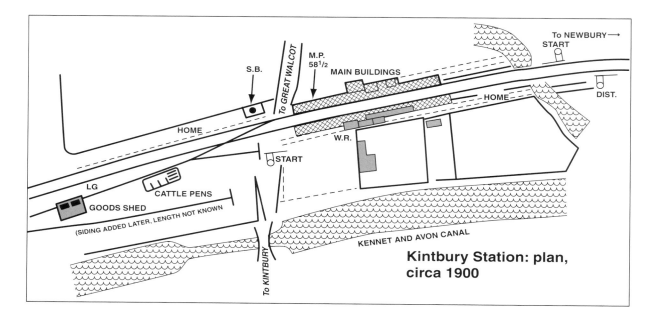

Kintbury Station: plan, circa 1900

more freight from the railway which by then was in the throes of nationalisation. By the 50s little was left but coal and there were was seldom more than three wagons in the yard. There was a single daily 'pick-up' freight train known as 'The Fly' – aptly named as it was always fly weight, dropping off one or possibly two wagons and collecting one or two coal empties. Sometimes it would simply pass through! So activity declined. I think the large crane was last used to unload concrete pipes for sewerage installation in the 50s and even then the pipes had come by road and the crane only used to off-load into contractors' vehicles.

Eventually the government of the day 'did something about it' and the renowned Beeching axe fell upon Kintbury. Thus on 7th September 1964 the freight yard was closed completely. Later on all the sidings were removed, the goods shed demolished and the crane cut up for scrap.

According to my 1902 timetable there were eight 'up' passenger trains and 12 'down' on most weekdays with three 'up' and two 'down' on Sundays. Most had connections with Paddington. Fares befitted the age and in new money are quoted as 51p, 33p and 26p respectively for singles from Hungerford to Paddington for first, second and third class. Kintbury fares would have been slightly less and returns were just under double the single fares. Today an ordinary return fare, Kintbury to Paddington is £25.80. The second class travel was abolished well before the first war but until comparatively recently categories continued to be referred to as 'first' and 'third'.

Until 1964 Kintbury station was fully staffed. My uncle

Lionel Gilbert started at Kintbury as a 'Lad Porter' in 1919 when there were two Porters and a Stationmaster working the station. In addition there were three signalmen who operated the signals and a gang of about six 'Platelayers' who looked after the track. The station was manned from about six in the morning until ten at night. The porters worked a shift system whereby one man worked the morning shift from six 'till about four o'clock in the afternoon. The other man would start at lunch time and work through till ten in the evening. The stationmaster lived adjacent the station in a tied house provided by the railway. He would appear at nine and finish at five approximately. The station staff would look after the passengers' needs (issuing tickets and information; dealing with luggage and parcels and keeping the place clean and tidy). They would also handle parcels and milk traffic using the passenger trains. They would also deal with the goods traffic at the goods yard handling the shunting of the 'fly' and any other wagons, help with loading and unloading as required and do all the clerical work. This was quite a heavy workload during the days of prosperity but tailed off quite a bit after the second world war. The signal box was manned on a 24 hour basis. The three signalmen working a three shift system. The platelayers worked a complex system which meant normal daytime working hours during weekdays with weekend working as required which could mean very long hours indeed, particularly during emergencies. I got to know the station and its working very well in the late 40s and 50s and spent many happy hours there as a railway enthusiast.

In those days there was a Mr. Helen as stationmaster and in addition to my uncle there was Alf Fitchett as the other porter. Two signalmen I can remember. One was Ernie Ansell who allowed me into the box and I was soon able to signal a train through all by myself but under his watchful eye. The other was a Mr. Hobbs. Eventually Mr. Helen moved on and towards the end there was no stationmaster and the duties became part of the Newbury stationmaster. Alf Fitchett retired and sadly lived only a few weeks in retirement. With the withdrawal of staff in 1964 Kintbury station became an 'unstaffed halt'. My uncle had two years to go before retirement and spent most of this time as a travelling ticket examiner which he greatly enjoyed. The signal box remained staffed 24 hours per day. In 1975 there was a rationalisation of the signalling arrangements. New continental-style lifting barriers replaced the old gates at Kintbury and at Hampstead Crossing. A new-low level signal box was erected on the south side of the line at Kintbury that controlled both level crossings which were equipped with television cameras etc. as is now pretty standard throughout Britain's railway network. The original box which probably dated back to the opening of the line was unceremoniously demolished and the gates cut up for scrap. At least one of the lamps still exists as it was re-erected in my garden eventually. Many tales were told by my uncle of the good old days when the Great Western Railway really meant something. Mostly these were about passenger eccentricities, minor derailments and train failures. Kintbury never hit the headlines with a major incident. I can remember during the war when a 'buffer locking' incident brought the mighty Cornish Riviera Express to a halt at Kintbury. After a long delay the King Class locomotive shunted the two buffer locked coaches into the goods yard before proceeding on its way. Long after my uncle had retired he was still taking phone calls at home from people wanting to know train times and of course being a railwayman of the old school he was able to oblige.

Kintbury goes into the Millennium as an unstaffed halt with minimal passenger facilities. A remote television monitor gives up-to-date train information but the very basic passenger shelters give scant protection from the icy blasts blowing across the water meadows. Today's services have actually *increased* with 16 'up' and 17 'down' trains weekdays and six each way on Sundays. More people than ever before travel constantly now – but not by rail. Will the railways ever assume the importance they had once? Can they ever make an impact upon the vast use of roads? The old goods yard has gone for ever, so has passenger parcel traffic. Much more positive efforts will have to made by government and the travelling public. Recent privatisation has had little effect to date so what will the next century bring? The railways of Britain have an illustrious past – but what of their future?

The Cornish Riviera Express passing the old Kintbury signal box.

My Days at the Post Office

by Kit Palmer

I was born at No. 1 The Cliffs, which my parents moved into shortly after this terrace was built by Mr. Harold Phillips, who owned Kintbury Mill as well as land and quite a few houses in the village.

I went to Kintbury St. Mary's School and Mr. Wilde was Headmaster then. He was very strict but a good teacher. He always kept his cane tucked up his sleeve – we children couldn't see it but we knew it was there. Because of that I don't think he had to use it often! In 1923 I left school and went to work in the post office. Mrs. Alice Kate Bance was Postmistress then. The office was in Station Road and outwardly as you can see from the photograph it looked much the same then as it does today. It is now a house but still called 'The Old Post Office'.

I was there for about five years and did all the usual postal duties. But I had one more and this was to operate the switchboard which controlled all the telephones in Kintbury – 33 of them! The system was manual and worked through a board where incoming calls were connected by cord and plug to the subscriber's number and likewise with outgoing calls. Not only that I had to time all long-distance calls and price them. I remember it was 2/– (10p) to London for three minutes. We had to give a 24-hour service so if the bell went in the middle of the night, then someone from the house had to get out of bed, go down to the office and deal with it. Not much fun on a cold winter's night with only a candle as there was no electricity then. The telephone system ran off batteries which were stored in a shed in the garden. Once a week someone from Hungerford came out to check these and top up the accumulators. It was not until the mid-30's that Kintbury was automated for subscribers, though calls were still dealt with manually at the Newbury Exchange.

We worked long hours then – from 8.00 a.m. to 7.00 p.m. We had our own Postmen too, who all lived in the village. They operated from the office where the post came in at about 6.00 a.m. and was then sorted into rounds. They were Freddy Colbourn, Benny Griffin, Tommy Kent and Alf Skinner (he was also the local tailor and ran his business from a shop just down the road – now Pound Cottage). They all did an early morning delivery and then a second one later. Whatever the weather, the first post always had to go out, even if they could not use their bikes and had to walk. With the second delivery, sometimes if things were really bad, there might be an instruction from Newbury not to go out but we could not make that decision ourselves. I always felt sorry for Tommy Kent because it was his job after he had done his morning rounds to cycle over to Combe in the afternoon to clear the postbox there and, on his way back, empty another box at Lower Green, Inkpen, then cycle on to Hungerford to hand in the mail before returning to Kintbury. Sometimes it was 7 o'clock in the evening before he got back home.

Besides answering the telephone we had many and varied jobs to do. Often we had to help out customers who were not very good at reading and writing. They would bring things in and ask us to read them out and to help them answer letters and compose telegrams. I particularly remember a family of gypsies who used to camp in the gravel pits up Mill Lane, who came in for help in this way.

The post office was always busy with people coming in to post letters and parcels, buy stamps and get their pensions. We had one gentleman who would come down on his horse and without dismounting would flick the window with his whip. This was a signal for one of us to go out and see what he wanted – which was usually stamps. I did this one day and Mrs. Bance caught me and wanted to know what I was doing. When I told her she ticked me off and said that this gentleman must come in and get his stamps like every other customer!

People sent a lot of telegrams in those days when phones were few and far between, and when these came in from elsewhere they had to be delivered and this was part of my job too – all for 2/6d. (12$\frac{1}{2}$p) a week – which is all I got when I first started work. At the end of each day all the outgoing mail was bagged up and taken on a handcart down to the station to go by passenger train to Newbury for sorting. It was not always just letters and parcels. People used to send game and poultry by mail just as they were – feathers and all – the only regulation was that the birds' heads had to be covered up!

In November 1928 I left Kintbury and sailed from Tilbury to Ceylon where I married George Palmer who was then serving as an instructor in the Ceylon Defence Force. We were out there until 1931, when my husband rejoined the Regular Army back in this country. However it was not until 1940, soon after the outbreak of the Second World War, that I returned to Kintbury and by 1942 I was back in the post office again, this time as Postmistress. This was on the retirement of Percy Bance who had taken over as Postmaster when his wife died early in 1929. A few things had changed on my return – the switchboard had gone and we had electricity. But we still had our postmen Freddy Colbourn, Benny Griffin, Tommy Kent and Alf Skinner.

Because it was wartime there was an extra job and this was selling National Savings Stamps and Certificates. I got very involved when we had a national 'Wings for Victory' week in 1943. We were in competition with Lambourn to see which village could raise the most money – and we won with £22,000 – a staggering amount for that time. I got special praise from Mrs. Monkhouse, one of the organisers, who lived at Forbury and later at Barrymores. She wasn't so pleased though with some people who had bought rather nice things at a local auction, paying for them by buying National Savings Stamps for the War Effort, only to come to the post office the next week to cash them in! And so life went on. The war ended and my husband George retired from the army in 1946. We were living in the house adjoining the post office, having moved there when I took over.

Whilst I was working, George kept himself busy getting involved with the village and this went on until his death in 1974. Among other things, he helped to set up and run a very active branch of the British Legion here, and this included the building of a clubhouse on land which is now part of Lawrencemead. Here many activities took place. There was a bar and probably the most popular thing was the dances held regularly and always packed out. With others he also started the Boys' Club in a hut near to the Legion. Not only that, he was also Chairman of the Parish Council for many years. I even found out some time afterwards that he used to 'drill' the local St. John Ambulance group – here his army Sergeant Major experience came in useful!

I retired as Postmistress in 1970 – after 28 years. No-one could be found who would take over the office and so it was transferred into the Corner Stores. Later it moved across the way to the newsagents on the corner of Inkpen Road (now converted into two cottages) and then back to the Corner Stores where it is today, run by Mr. Johal.

Eventually I sold my home which by then had become the 'Old Post Office' and moved to my present home in The Croft.

Looking back, it has been a good life and I would not have missed my days in the post office, especially the early ones!

The old Post Office in Station Road, early 1920s.

Head Parlourmaid, Landgirl and Tea with Sir Terence

by 'Sis' Braidwood

When my family first came to these parts they lived at Denford and my father worked at Avington. Dad was known as 'Fishy' by most people and this was because at one time he worked for his father who ran a fish stall. Anyway, just before the First War they moved to Kintbury Farm cottages where I was born and which are now part of the farmhouse. Here he worked on the farm for Mr. Lawrence and then after a while he got a job working on the farm and in the garden for Miss Peglar at Barrymores. We all moved into the lodge at the drive entrance which is now Malford Lodge. We were a big family for I had three sisters and four brothers.

I went to St. Mary's School and when I was about 13, in the holidays I used to get up about 6 o'clock in the morning, go up to Barrymores, across two fields and fetch in six cows. Then I helped Dad wash them down, milk them and then turn them out again into the fields. Then it was back to the cowshed to wash it down; after that into the garden to help with weeding and other jobs. I had things to do for my mother too. Monday was wash day, so early in the morning with my sister Joan we took an old pram down the track to Titcomb to collect wood for the copper fire. Of all days I liked Sunday best because it was then we had cake for tea – other days it was usually bread and lard sprinkled with sugar!

When I left school I had a few different jobs. One was at Newbury Laundry and I think I must have been there for about four years. There were five of us Kintbury girls and we used to cycle there and back in all sorts of weather. I also worked for a short while at Kirby House, Inkpen. This was a job that Dad got me. I was a daily maid and cycled there and back too. It was £1 a month, one day off each month and a half day off each Sunday – except I had to go back for 7 o'clock in the evening. I also worked for Mrs. Lawrence at Prospect House. Here I was a 'living-in maid' with my own bedroom and I was there for a while.

It wasn't all work though. When there were things going on in the village and around that we fancied, we went along. Most popular were the Friday night 'Sixpenny Hops' in the Coronation Hall. They were packed out usually and we danced away to music provided by a pianist and some other instrument, probably a saxophone. In the summer there were fêtes and at one I remember going in for 'Catching the Pig': and I caught it after chasing it over two fields. The prize was the pig which we took down to the butcher to be slaughtered and this provided us with a fair number of good meals. A the same fête my mother was lucky too, for she caught the cockerel in another chasing race. Soon after, these kind of races were banned as they were considered cruel.

My sister Win and I were getting fed up with Kintbury so we decided to go to London where we got 'living-in' jobs in the same house working for Lady Stewart – Win as Under-Housemaid and me as Under-Parlourmaid. Two years later she was Head Housemaid and I was Head Parlourmaid. By that time I wanted a move, so I went to Maidenhead where I had an aunt and where I went into service again. I had another interest here as I had a boyfriend who later became my husband. But before we married I decided to come back to Kintbury and I got my old job back with Mrs. Lawrence – and my old bedroom too! She also employed a Cook-General who lived in, so the two of us looked after the Lawrence family – Mr. and Mrs. and Miss Winifred. They had other staff who worked outside and in the business. Of these I remember Bob Hopkins who did odd jobs then and Mr. Ewins who worked in the office in the old barn (now a house) and helped run the family business of corn, coal merchant and farmer.

In 1939 I got married and moved away, but not for long, as my husband was called up and I returned to Kintbury again. It was not long before I was called up too. I was told either I had to join the Womens' Forces or become a Landgirl – which I decided to do. I was sent to Reading for training but they didn't keep me for long as I picked things up pretty quickly having done a bit of farmwork before I left school. I was sent to work for Mrs. Goodhart to work on the farm and in the garden. There were six cows to look after and to milk in the morning and again at 4 o'clock in the afternoon. In between it was work in the garden. There was another landgirl there as well. Nothing very exciting happened excepting that one day when we were working near the lake a small boy fell in and we had to wade in and rescue him. I left there when I was expecting my daughter Jean and then later on I had twin boys, Michael and Paul.

By this time the war was over and from time to time I did odd jobs like fruit picking in the gardens on the Craven Estate. That was before the gardens and the estate yard were sold and all the buildings there converted into houses. After that I went to work at Barton Court when it was a boys' boarding school – Purton Stoke. I worked in the kitchen garden and in the grounds. Eventually the

Barton Court, Kintbury. C+S R (C)

school left and after a while Sir Terence Conran came to live there and it was a private house once more. The gardens became much more interesting then, as Sir Terence had his own ideas how he wanted them to be, especially the kitchen garden in which he took a particular interest. It is lovely now and provides vegetables and especially herbs for his London restauarants. Sir Terence is a nice man who enjoys his visits to Barton Court at weekends. Sometimes, if he was in the garden, he would say to me "Come on Sis – let's go and have a cup of tea".

My memories of life in Kintbury in the 20's and 30's are mixed. We had some good times – especially at the dances; but one that I don't care to think about was when our family had to move and we couldn't find anywhere to go except some terrible houses, shacks really, long since demolished in Pig Lane (Laylands Green). They belonged to a man who lived in Newbury Street and everyone knew how bad they were. They only had earth floors but we still had to pay 2/– a week rent. My sister and I shared a bed and we could lie there and look out and see across the fields through a crack in the wall. Not only that, they were rat infested and we even had them running over our bed. This would have been about 1936 and fortunately the Council were building new houses and we were moved into the first one as soon as it was ready. Even there we had no electricity at first though it was put in fairly soon after. It had no bathroom and only an earth closet and we had to wait until well after the war for this to be put right.

Of all the jobs I had, my 32 years at Barton Court were the most enjoyable and I was sad when the time came for me to finally retire. However, I made some really good friends down there and I still go back most Wednesday mornings to see what is going on and to have a cup of tea.

Kintbury Coronation Village Hall

by Tony Hopgood

1911 was the year of the Coronation of King George V. On Monday, 6th April 1911 a public meeting was held in the village school (now St Mary's House) at which it was decided by 20 votes to 2 to build a Coronation Hall. A committee of worthy gentlemen was formed – no ladies in those days – and it was agreed to try and purchase some land. On Monday, 1st May Mr. Humphrey Walmesley owner of Inglewood and his son told the committee that they had identified some land which could be purchased for £130: they offered this land as a gift. The committee were delighted but when they went to inspect the site they found to their horror that it was too big. After some negotiation the site was reduced to 103 feet by 80 feet and the price came down to £82.10s.0d. Mr. Walmesley and his son were not prepared to have their generosity slighted: they offered the balance of the original sum as a contribution to the building costs.

The committee then asked Mr. Hill, a Newbury architect, to draw up plans for a hall to seat 250 people. Plans were produced and a size of 53 feet by 25 feet was agreed – hardly big enough for 250 people, but perhaps there were to be no stage or gangways. Tenders were sought and the lowest bid came from Mr. Bance of Ball Hill, the quoted price being £697. The next step was predictable: the committee asked what Mr. Bance could do to reduce his price. Well, yes, if he used cheaper ventilators, no panelling and cheap local plain tiles for the roof, the price could come down to £606.9s.7d!

In June the committee resolved "That the Parish Council should not be asked to take over the Hall until it is free from debt and the present committee should stand until this was done". Brave words!

Soon afterwards the committee went to the field to stake out the Hall. They decided to place it 20 feet from the road rather than 25 feet so as to leave five feet at the rear for later expansion: very far sighted even if five feet was rather small.

Things moved quickly in those days: by 21st August building was underway and it was ready to be opened by Sir Richard Sutton at 3 p.m. on 12th February 1912. The opening ceremony was followed by a concert with another concert taking place in the evening. Profits on the first day were £13.13s.0d.

Fund raising continued, but in July 1912 the builder was still owed £200 and already there were demands for further expenditure to replace oil lamps with electric lights. The first World War led to the Hall not being used so much and revenue fell: it was not until 1921 that the debt had been nearly cleared and the debate opened on whether or not the Hall should become the responsibility of the Parish Council. By 1923 this idea had been rejected and a constitution was approved which established the Hall as a Trust with a set of rules and regulations.

The 1923 constitution remained in force until 1968 when a new scheme was established by the Secretary of State of Education and Science under section 18 of the Charities Act 1960.

The original structure was a fairly basic building, its only refinement being two coke stoves on the Eastern wall. Over the succeeding years various improvements were made: the Committee Room was built and later divided into two areas to provide space for a kitchen; toilets were built at the Southern end of the Hall and a stage erected at the Northern end – it partly blocked the main entrance! The original floor comprising 9 inch pine planks must have been very difficult to keep clean: it was covered in the 1950s with a polished strip maple floor – this explains why there is a change in level as you enter the Hall. The maple floor then suffered from impact of stiletto heels and was then sanded so often that it had to be replaced with a new surface in 1995. The maple floor covers the bases of the coke stoves, so it is likely that a large bore radiator system was installed when the maple floor was first laid.

By 1977 the village was beginning to grow rapidly and attention turned to the requirements of the enlarged population. Several thousand pounds had been collected to commemorate the Silver Jubilee of Queen Elizabeth II and a proposal was made to spend this sum, together with the proceeds of the sale of the Coronation Hall, on a new community facility. Such were the emotional feelings towards the old Hall that there was an outcry against this idea and subsequent deliberations generated proposals both to build a new hall for sport and to modernise the Coronation Hall. In the event, priority was given to the building of the Jubilee Centre whilst the major improvements to the Coronation Hall had to wait another ten years.

The major improvements proved to be very eventful: basically there was a need to make the Hall compliant with current standards. This demanded a new kitchen, new toilets and a toilet for the disabled. Various plans were prepared and the one finally agreed moved the stage to the southern end of the Hall, had good backstage provision, a chair store, a substantial store room for the Play Group together with other store cupboards. The Committee Room returned to its original size with the removal of the old kitchen. Tenders were obtained, a contractor chosen, a contract placed and a substantial down payment made. No sooner had the work started and the roof opened up when the contractor went bankrupt. There then began an heroic effort by a team of volunteers, working with skills they did not know they had, to make the Hall weatherproof and to get the extensions completed in a situation where there was a gross shortage of cash. The village owes a great debt to everyone involved in this dramatic venture which was completed in 1991 at a cost of £125,000.

There remained a shortage of cash and for several years thereafter the Hall was cleaned – to a very high standard – by a team of volunteers. Fund raising activities were initiated: fortnightly whist and bingo raised sums approaching £1,000 a year and these were later supplemented with Quiz Nights and an Annual Fête run at the same time as the Horticultural Society's Flower Show. As funds improved and with substantial support from Miss Lawrence's Trust, the District Council and the Parish Council, it became possible to landscape the land around the Hall and provide parking for 39 cars. This was completed in 1994 at a cost of £30,000 with the kitchen facilities being later enhanced with new cookers and worktops being donated by the Volunteer Group and use by the hard of hearing being helped by the provision of a Loop System provided by Meridian Television.

The one part of the Hall not upgraded in the major improvements was the Committee Room. By 1997 the revenue from letting the Hall had risen to over £10,000 a year, substantially covering the running costs and providing funds for further facilities. With support from Miss Lawrence's Trust, the District Council and the Parish Council, this enabled a soundproof wall to be built to isolate the Committee Room from the Hall with the additional benefit of providing a stage lighting control room and a substantial cupboard. New lighting, carpet and quality furniture transformed the Committee Room into a very pleasing environment.

These facilities themselves would be worth nothing if they were not used. In fact use of the Hall is such that there are typically four or five bookings a day. Over 20 village organisations use the Hall on a regular basis: some have been using the Hall for a generation or more and some have recently been formed. Of particular significance was the formation in the early 1970s of St Mary's Drama Group, by the vicar's wife Christine Millard, and the Kintbury Players, by Dorothy Miller. These two organisations established a strong tradition of plays, revues and pantomime which utilise the Hall for a dozen or more performances a year. Daytime use of the Hall is dominated by the activities of the pre-school Play Group

The Coronation Hall when first built.

and by Adult Education under the auspices of Newbury College, which concentrate on art classes and upholstery classes. Monthly village lunches, served by the Volunteer Group, are very popular. At weekends, there is a strong demand for use of the Hall by private parties and every year a number of wedding receptions are held.

In many respects the Coronation Hall is the centre of village activity: it is a great credit to all the men and women who have served on the Hall Management Committee throughout the century and everyone else who has given freely of their time to develop and maintain the Hall that it is so well used today.

This history is based on original research done by Doreen Anstey

Flower Shows and Fêtes

by Heather Turner

Kintbury's first Garden Society came about in the 1880s so by 1900 it was well established. Known as 'Kintbury Cottage Garden Society' it existed purely to organise the Annual Flower Show, usually held in August and combined with a very popular Sports Day, the latter having a considerable reputation throughout the district according to reports in the Newbury Weekly News of that time.

The 1914-18 War saw the temporary demise of the show and efforts to revive it afterwards were not particularly successful, until we come to 1924 and this must have seen it at its peak. Col. Walmesley, who lived at Inglewood Lodge and had a reputation as a 'first class organiser', took a hand and things really got under way once more. The show was held in a field adjoining his home known by locals at that time as the 'Flower Show Meadow'. Soldiers from Tidworth Barracks put on a splendid display, ladies took part in a 'Catch the Pig' race, prize being the young pig and there was to have been a 'Chicken race' but the forerunner of the R.S.P.C.A. threatened to prosecute if they detected cruelty, so this idea was abandoned. Children's races of every imaginable description were held and there were very large entries – most families were big in those days!

The Flower Show itself was interesting. There were classes for 'Labourers' and also for 'Others' which would have included the 'Gentry', many of whom employed gardeners. Exhibits were mainly vegetables and fruit, with a few flowers thrown in. Ladies were not forgotten as they could compete with 'dishes of boiled potatoes, knitted socks'– and the piece de resistance 'making a man's shirt'. Other curios included 'A collection of Queen Wasps' – prize going to the highest number – presumably dead, not alive!

Teas were organised and this was taken very seriously, the committee comprising over 20 people and a stipulation that all ingredients must be bought locally. Cars were not much in evidence in 1924 but facilities were provided for bicycle parking and receipts are recorded for 130 paid-up bikes. The show was held on a Wednesday afternoon concluding in the evening with dancing on Col. Walmesley's lawn.

Prominent village people served on the various show committees and such names as Alison, Chislett, Dopson,

Ewens Rennie and Randall will be remembered by some today. However the revival did not last long and in 1930 the Society was wound up through lack of interest.

It was not until 1958 that the present Horticultural Society came into being. Founders were Henry Kingscott and Oswald Smith following a meeting called in Henry's bedroom – he not being very well at the time. It differed from the earlier Society in that not only does it run an Annual Show, classes being very different, but holds regular meetings with visits and demonstrations throughout the year. Today it has over 150 members including many from Hungerford and surrounding villages. As such it is one of our most thriving groups. Oswald Smith – known always as 'O.H.' was Chairman for many years, succeeded by Allan Wells and then by present chairman, Peter Moreton.

Though there was a lapse of some 28 years between the two societies much gardening went on here in the intervening years, especially during the 30s. The big houses still had their gardeners, notably Barton Court, Elcot Park, Inglewood and Wallingtons. Council houses built in the 20s and 30s had extremely long gardens cultivated to provide vegetables for their families. In addition there were no less than six large allotment sites including two near the station specifically for employees of the old G.W.R. Houses occupy most of this land now but part of the former Station Road allotments remains where plots are actively cultivated today by a new generation of keen gardeners.

Fêtes have been very much part of Kintbury life during the century. Apart from those run over the years in conjunction with the Flower Shows they have been held to celebrate, entertain and to raise money. Notable occasions within living memory have been the Silver Jubilee of King George V in 1935 when the Eighteenth Century Kintbury Fire Engine (currently being stored by the West Berks Museum) was decorated patriotically and pulled by local lads in the procession and houses were decorated with red, white, and blue bunting and flowers. Then, celebrations after the 1939-45 War and a second Silver Jubilee, that of Queen Elizabeth II in 1978, from which emerged the annual Street Fayre which continues today.

Early Fêtes were big events, usually including a local Silver Band from East Woodhay, Inkpen or elsewhere. Showmen provided such excitements as 'Swingboats' and a variety of sideshows for which they gave a small donation or a bit more 'if they had a good day'. Baby Shows were a feature – judges consisting of local professional and prominent people – the 1924 classes being decided by Dr. Leggat from Newbury, Nurse Jordan who will still be remembered by quite a few people – as will her bike and 'District Nurse' manner – truly one of the old school! Third judge was Mrs. Mahon of Barton Gables. Fêtes continue in Kintbury today, usually organised by our various local groups – and each with its own special character and purpose.

KINTBURY and AVINGTON.

THE FORTY-FOURTH

Cottage Garden Show

AND SPORTS

WILL BE HELD AT

INGLEWOOD LODGE

(By kind permission), on

Wednesday, August 20th, 1924

Commencing TWO p.m.

ATTRACTIONS –

MILITARY DISPLAY

AND VARIOUS SIDE SHOWS.

PRICES OF ADMISSION :

2 to 5 o'clock, Adults 1/2 (including Tax) ; Children 6d.
After 5 o'clock, Adults, 9d. (including Tax) ; Children 3d.

BLACKET TURNER & CO. LTD., PRINTERS, NEWBURY.

Kintbury's Drama Groups

by Doreen Anstey

In the autumn of 1972 a new Vicar and his wife arrived in Kintbury. Little did we realise that this event was to make such an impact on the lives of young and old in the village.

The Reverend Albert and Mrs. Christine Millard came to us from the Parish of Crookham and the grapevine told us that Mrs. Millard was very keen on Drama – what an understatement! We were soon to learn that Christine was an extremely talented pianist and song writer, an able writer of pantomimes, revue sketches, competition drama and religious drama.

Her love of children and young people was rapidly shown. The village Youth Club was flagging and needed a stimulus; so in stepped Christine and the first Revue was born and so was the St. Mary's Drama Group. The Vicar acted as Treasurer (although there was very little money) and Christine was Producer and general organiser. The Mother's Union and members of the church congregation and anyone who could contribute in any way were all roped in to help.

The Vicar supported Christine in all her ventures and being himself an able actor was roped into her productions; and so the vicarage became the hub of the drama group, rehearsals were held there, sewing was done there, production meetings were held there and at show times the spare bedrooms were full of costumes and props.

The next stage was the first pantomime – Aladdin – performed over the New Year period 1973/74. The group had no money to speak of so people were asked to turn out their wardrobes and cupboards for their old evening clothes, curtains and any suitable material for costumes. One lady was heard to remark "That the Princess looked lovely in her mother's cut-down dress". White sheets were used to make the peasant blouses and they are still in use today over 25 years later. It was very good sheeting – boilable!

Having read the history of the Agricultural Riots in Kintbury, Christine decided the subject would make a very good competition play. With the help of Mr. and Mrs. B. Shawyer, who did the research into the true facts and details, the play was written, produced and off went the cast, scenery, costumes, props etc., not forgetting the supporters, to the Maidenhead Drama Festival. A very prestigious Festival with an extremely high standard. The play won first in its class and we came away with

honours. The play was also featured on BBC TV South.

The group entered the Maidenhead Festival four times and in each case we always came back with honours, especially in the Community Theatre section when, on one occasion, we could have been in the National Finals.

Getting to Maidenhead was always an achievement in itself: a cast of forty five, large pieces of scenery for the large stage transported by lorry; costumes, props; six very large silver serving dishes and covers, helpers and supporters. Panic as we were held up in the traffic, but we somehow always made the stage on time.

It was thanks to the hard work and dedication of Christine that we enjoyed so much success. She was a perfectionist and a hard task master, but a joy to work with and her casts, young and old, always tried to attain the highest standard possible.

During the year we did a revue, festival play and pantomime; Christine also produced the St Mary's Church Fol de Rols and religious dramas. Any monies made by these productions was ploughed back into the Coronation Hall. We had to buy new chairs for our patrons to sit on, a new piano, cups and saucers and odds and ends, but it was fun and enjoyed by all participants.

In early 1976 there arrived in the Village another dedicated theatrical lady. Mrs. Dorothy Miller came with her daughter and son-in-law, Margaret and Alan Barr, to live in the Old School in Church Street. Mrs. Miller had been producer of a very successful group in Caterham where six plays per year were performed in a theatre named after her. A meeting was arranged between Mrs. Miller, Mrs. Millard and representatives from the Evening Women's Institute Drama section and it was agreed Mrs. Miller form a group to perform straight plays – two per year – Christine to produce revues, pantomimes and festival plays and the WI would just do competition work.

The name Kintbury Players was chosen by Dorothy and the first play was performed in the autumn of 1976: "Lloyd George knew my Father" which was a great success. The group went from strength to strength and although Dorothy has now passed away the group still flourishes. Since 1976 they have presented 29 plays, four revues – one of them especially for the Jubilee – and three in conjunction with St. Mary's group.

The St. Mary's group still enjoys their involvement with young people and although revues are off the calendar at this point in time, due in part to finding a pianist who can cope with the singing voices, the panto still goes on. The young members section, called Benchmark Theatre, entered a play in the Hungerford Community Arts Festival, so carrying on a tradition.

*The Rev. Albert and
Christine Millard,
founders of the
St. Mary's Drama Group.*

*Taking a bow; the cast
of "The Snow Queen"
pantomime 1999.*

Miss Lawrence

A Village Benefactress

Over recent years, many village groups have benefited from grants made by the 'Lawrence Trust'. These include grants towards the refurbishment of the Coronation Hall, St. Mary's School, The Friends of St. Mary's Tower Appeal, the Kintbury Volunteer Group and Kintbury Youth Club among others. All recipients of these grants have been most grateful, but younger people may wonder who was Miss Lawrence?

Winifred Edith Lawrence, born 1896, was the only child of Arthur and Rachel Lawrence. Some years before her birth Mr. Lawrence started a corn merchant's business in Kintbury and later a coal merchant's, and these businesses flourished. The family lived at Prospect House, Station Road, a house with a very large garden. As was usual at the time, Mr. Lawrence conducted his business from home with offices on Station Road attached to one of the three large barns he used for storing and threshing the grain. In addition, Mr. Lawrence owned Kintbury Farm and allotment land adjoining the coal yard, and fields to the rear of Prospect House.

After the death of her parents in 1942 and 1943, Miss Lawrence continued to live at Prospect House. Eventually she disposed of the family's business interests, retaining the farm and land holdings. Winifred Lawrence is remembered as a very kind woman, shy but supportive of many village activities. She was President of the St. Mary's Drama Group in its early days, and was also a founder member of the British Floral Design Society, and was a generous patron of local art exhibitions. She had an abiding love of gardening, birds and animals.

Miss Lawrence spent all her life at Prospect House and when she died aged 82, apart from generous legacies to her family and friends, she left £100,000 to the National Trust and the residue of her estate to a trust – the Miss W.E. Lawrence 1973 Charitable Settlement – from which Kintbury's community has benefited. Thank you, Miss Lawrence.

Winifred Lawrence (left) *with her cousin Vera Hull, outside Prospect House.*

The Lawrence Fields on the left.

The Kennet & Avon Canal

by Sybil Flinn

The Kennet & Avon Canal forms a boundary across the northern side of the village. This 200-year-old waterway is a feature of village life. Babies are pushed in prams along the towpath, children feed ducks, sweethearts stroll together, anglers fish, older people take constitutionals, and everyone uses it as an indicator when giving directions – "off the A4, over the canal and . . .".

It is difficult to believe that in 1955 the canal was to be scheduled for closure, which, had it taken place, would by now have reduced this waterway to a filled-in depression. What happened?

First a little history. In the late 18th century, the Kennet & Avon Canal was designed as the only waterway across the south of England to link London, via the Thames, with Bristol in the west, then the country's busiest port. Two sections, the Avon Navigation (a short section at Bristol), and the Kennet Navigation, from Reading to Newbury, had been completed earlier and a proposal to link Bath with Newbury received Parliamentary approval as the Kennet & Avon Canal Act in 1794.

An early Kintbury link was the appointment of Mr. Charles Dundas, who lived at Barton Court, as Chairman of the Kennet & Avon Canal Company. Mr. Dundas served as Chairman for 38 years, was created Baron Amesbury, and his memorial may be seen in St. Mary's Church. John Rennie, only 29 years old, but already a skilled engineer, was responsible for the design of the project. Work started in October 1794, and the first section to be completed in 1797 was the section from Newbury to Kintbury, the opening of which was celebrated in great style.

The total Kennet & Avon Canal system consists of 87 miles of canal, 104 locks, two aqueducts, a tunnel of almost 500 metres and two pumping stations. The summit of the canal is at Crofton, where the beam engines used to raise the water for the canal, remain the oldest working beam engines in the world. At Devizes, the canal descends 237 feet down the hillside via a staircase of 29 locks. It was a marvellous feat of construction achieved by the simple means available at that time, mainly manpower.

The Kintbury section runs 2¾ miles from the parish boundary at Hungerford Common, through three locks – Wire, Brunsdon's and Kintbury – to the boundary with Hamstead Marshall, between the Wilderness and Irish

The late Miss Winifred Rennie, great-great-grand-daughter of John Rennie, engineer of the Kennet & Avon Canal, re-opens Kintbury Lock in 1972.

Hill. The River Kennet interlaces with the canal, and with the water meadows to the north, this makes the Kintbury section a particularly beautiful part of the whole waterway.

There is no doubt that the building of the canal was an asset to Kintbury. A wharf was constructed opposite the 'Dundas Arms' and from the completion of the sections linking Kintbury with Newbury, and then to Hungerford, there was a busy trade in the transport of goods to and from Kintbury itself. Coal, the basic fuel for everyone came from South Wales. In turn timber was carried and the output from Kintbury's whiting industry.

Kintbury people would have become familiar with the sight of the large broad-beamed canal barges carrying 60 tons fully laden – almost twice the maximum load of present-day road haulage. Each barge had a small rear cabin, living accommodation for the bargee *and* his family. The barges were towed by horses walking the towpath, and the average time for transit from Newbury to Bristol was three days, nine hours. Nothing at the time could match this transporting capacity.

For a brief half-century the canal trade flourished – and then came the railway. In 1841 the Great Western Railway line between Bristol and London was built, and materials for the construction were hauled by canal, but the completion of the line resulted in a loss of most of the through traffic for the Kennnet & Avon.

Kintbury, with its position on the main line was able to adapt quickly to the railway age. The wharf, with its back to the railway, could be used for the trans-shipment of goods, and the land west of the wharf became the railway's goods yard, and our chapter 'Getting There' describes the many uses this served.

In 1851 the canal was acquired by the G.W.R. and from then on total control and policy was in railway hands. When taking over the K. & A. the railway had to guarantee to maintain the navigation, and the G.W.R. fulfilled its obligation by employing a lock-keeper for each section of the canal. However, little was allowed for major maintenance work and the passage through to Newbury eventually became impassable.

An interesting cargo at the end of the last century was when Mr. H. J. Walmesley, then owner of Inglewood, and a staunch catholic, had the chapel of his Lancashire home dismantled and brought piecemeal to Kintbury by canal barge. The chapel was then rebuilt at Inglewood.

Despite the loss of trade, the canal continued to serve one useful purpose at Kintbury for the first half of the twentieth century. Watercress, from the beds situated between the canal and the Hungerford Road, which continued to be cultivated until the 1960s, was bunched and packed in baskets. These were then loaded on to a punt and taken down the canal to the railway station, where it was dispatched to markets in London and Birmingham. Several men in Kintbury remember as boys, helping Dick Mills, the last watercress grower, with this task.

In 1955 the British Transport Commission (now in control of the nationalised railways), decided to apply to Parliament for abandonment of the entire Kennet & Avon Canal system. The announcement brought immediate reaction from the Kennet & Avon Canal Association, a local conservation body formed some years earlier. It was decided to organise a public petition against the closure. Signing the petition was limited to those who were living

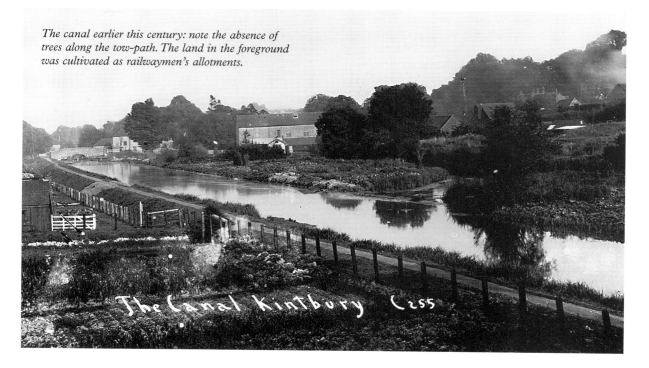

The canal earlier this century: note the absence of trees along the tow-path. The land in the foreground was cultivated as railwaymen's allotments.

along the canal, or had a direct interest in the waterway. Even so, the response was immediate: 20,000 signatures were collected and on 28th January 1956, a great crowd of supporters assembled to accompany the petition to London. The petition, bound in two large leather volumes, was taken to London by canoe down the waterway, carried overland where the canal was impassable. The supporters had been encouraged to dress according to their interest in the waterway, and so a very large crowd of bargees, fishermen, yachtsmen, farmers etc. walked through the London streets carrying the petition to the Ministry in Berkeley Square. This attracted enormous press and TV coverage.

The petition was successful and the bill for closure was withdrawn. The government appointed a committee to look into the canal's future and the verdict was 'pre-eminently a case for redevelopment'.

From then onwards it was a partnership of the Kennet & Avon Canal Trust, the local authorities, and canal related businesses, working with British Waterways, which brought about the restoration of the waterway. It was to take 28 years, far longer than the original construction time. The Kintbury section which had been kept in water due to the inflow of the River Kennet, was in better shape than other parts. Wire Lock was the earliest lock to be restored, closely followed by Brunsdon's.

Eventually the work of restoration was complete. On 8th August 1990, the Queen opened the restored waterway in a ceremony at Devizes. After restoration it was apparent that more funds were needed to ensure the water supply, correct leakage and stability problems, and improve public access. In 1995 the restoration partnership made a bid for £25 million to the Heritage Lottery Fund. In 1996 this bid was granted, the largest grant at that time, and there is currently a six-year programme of work in hand, which will achieve a very long-term future for the waterway.

Restoration of this east-west passage has brought a constant progress of privately-owned narrow boats and hire craft to the canal and Kintbury. Summer sees many boat-going holidaymakers exploring Kintbury with shopping bags in hand. The unwary resident quietly enjoying the passing scene must field the enquiries – "where can I buy bread . . . a warm sweater . . . insect repellant . . . find a dentist?"

The Kennet & Avon Canal is alive and well, ably managed and maintained by British Waterways, whose lengthsmen can be seen on the job at Kintbury most days, adjusting sluices, checking locks, and guarding against flooding downstream. It is our linear park to enjoy – and we do!

It is a sign of spring and summer on the way when the horse-boat 'Kennet Valley' arrives at Kintbury shortly after Easter for another season of excursion and charter trips on the canal. This enterprise has been run by the Kennet Horse-Boat Company owned by Mr. and Mrs. Bob Butler since 1974.

The 'Kennet Valley' is a traditionally painted broad-beamed canal boat which will carry 76 passengers and the horse-power comes from shire-cross horses Hanna and Boncella in the charge of boatman John Head, who was coincidentally born in Kintbury, although he now lives elsewhere.

The horses work alternate days towing the boat to Hamstead Marshall or Hungerford. Hanna was the third horse bought to work since the Kintbury trips started. She caused some consternation shortly after starting work when she produced a foal, Boncella, which means an unexpected gift in Swahili. However, all was well and when she was adult, Boncella was able to join her mother on duty, in place of Queenie who was retired.

A horse-boat needs a crew of two; one to steer and the other to walk the horse who is pulling the barge by tow-line. There is no other power source. An emergency stop – sometimes needed when the barge is approached by inexperienced boaters on the wrong side – is executed by turning the barge's bows into the bank! 'Kennet Valley' attracts several hundred people each year, brought by coach from many parts of the south of England, to sample canal travel as it used to be.

We show John Head with Hanna and her daughter Boncella ('Bonnie').

The Craven Hunt at Wawcott

by Diane McBride

The Craven Hunt Kennels were originally based at Ashdown House, Lambourn (now a National Trust property), but early this century Lord Craven and Sir Richard Sutton joined together and set up the kennels, stables and housing for the hunt at Little Wawcott. The horses, staff and hounds were brought across from Lambourn and the hunt's new home became Wawcott. Stan Dance, who has lived in the farm cottages at Wawcott all his life, remembers that in those days they hunted three times a week or more throughout the season.

During 1936-1939 Stan spent any free time he had out of school at the kennels. Major Roydd was the Master at that time and he lived at Wawcott House. Stan used his bicycle to follow the Huntsman and the hounds setting off around 4.30 a.m. to wherever the meet was to start that day, sometimes quite close-by; like the Dundas Arms or Orpenham Farm, but it could be as far as Lambourn. Everyone hacked over to the meet in those days – there were no horse trailers or boxes and Stan remembers being

often soaking wet and cold, even before the day's hunting had started. The hunt would be out all day and would sometimes return as late as 9.30 p.m. At the end of the day, they would sound the horn as they returned home and gradually all the lamps would be lit in the kennels and the stables, and the stable lads would carry their lamps outside to light the way back for the horses. As the hounds returning from the day's hunt barked in excitement, those that had been left that day would sing and bark in reply.

There were between 12 and 20 stable lads working for the Hunt and they would all share the jobs, taking it in turn to cook for each other, and all sleeping in a large room above the mess room. Their duties included mucking out and exercising the horses, but Stan was often plonked on top of a horse without even a saddle and sent off round the field to exercise one of the hunters.

The pack of hounds plus the puppies were kept in the kennels, where no expense was spared for their comfort. There was even underfloor heating in the kennels operated by steam. The puppies were kept in separate pens and were allowed to run around the fields on their own. One day, the farm workers, who were working for Frank Moore had some work to do in the fields next to where the puppies were let out. They hung up their jackets and dinner bags and got on with their morning's work. When lunch-time came, they all hungrily reached for their bags, only to find

The Craven Hunt sets off from Wawcott in the 19. One of the riders is the then Master, John Player.

the puppies had stolen every scrap of food they could find! There was a slaughterhouse at the kennels and a paddock where farm animals, including horses, were kept until needed to feed the hounds.

There were many happy times to remember before the Second World War. Every Christmas, the Master held a big party for all the staff and their families. There was plenty of beer for the adults and lemonade for the children and good bread, cheese and beef to eat. Everyone mixed well and had a thoroughly good time and the children left with a small present, singing and laughing as they walked home across the fields.

Hunter Trials were always held at Wawcott Farm in the rickyard and Stan Dance remembers the course so well, he could still walk around it. The blacksmith, Frank Dobson, used to make the jumps; some were poles, some fir branches. Stan remembers them as being much higher than those seen today. Frank Charles Moore (known as Charlie) told Stan that if he was able to run and jump over the finished height of a fence, then that was the right height for his horses!

At the beginning of May every year, at the end of the season, all the horses were taken down to Kintbury Station, put on the train and sent away to the sales. When the new season started, a new batch of horses were brought in. It was rare to see the same horse two seasons running.

In the 1930s a new master arrived – John Player (of Player's Cigarettes family) – he still holds the record for the Craven Hunt of 102 brace of fox in one season, but after only a few seasons the war started and that meant an end more or less to hunting. However, Frank Moore (Charlie's father), who was a great huntsman, formed a committee to keep everything going as far as possible while the war went on. The pack of hounds was reduced to about a third in number, and with a skeleton staff of those over 45 or younger lads exempt from call-up, he kept the hunt going. Frank Moore spent nearly all his time walking the hounds and exercising the horses while his son, Charlie Moore, looked after the farm. Certainly if it had not been for Frank Moore's dedication the Craven Hunt may not have survived the war.

In the late 1940s the Craven Hunt moved from Wawcott and went to Membury where, after a few seasons, they amalgamated with the Vine. They are now based at Hannington. All the original buildings at Wawcott still stand, with the exception of two cottages which burnt down and the kennels where there is now a wood yard.

Poem for the Millennium

Some Misty Kintbury

Who tires of toiling by the Kennet, chalk and trout
Is left to grapple grayling, worm or fly.
Each evening, just as one of many groups
Squat down to poor man's salmon, focus eyes
On new stars from the Chorus to a Pantomime of Lights,
Their Coronation Hall continues to delight.

Last Millennium, some dozens down by the crossings
Safe from floodings from the delitescent Meadows,
Six Sisters courting the favours of Christ;
Crows on the Mead Bench scoffing pies,
And to this last the Faithful are measured on fingers
As those few lines encrypted in Doomsday.

> For Village life can be unkind
> Far better seek to find
> *Some Ambridge of the Mind*

This Village ticks a pace no longer measured by Seasons
Chalk rubbed out and Canal plied only for pleasures

> For *Flower Festival* or *Crafty Raft*
> For *Street Fayre* all its Froth & Fret

This ground steeped holiness one thousand years
Rest ancient Saxon bones
By Norman doorway & a chancel arch.

From Sarum up to Oxford's spires
From Bristol's Port to London on the Old Bath Road
Rests Halfway House, pretty as a pot.

In this Village as this Century turns
Just ring your wish on the New Bell's Tower:
All knowledge lies within your power
There's nothing which you cannot will to learn.

SNOWDEN BARNETT
August 1999

The Dunn family of Kintbury

by Piers Dunn

The Dunn family who settled in Kintbury in the 1820s had in the early years of this century started to go their different ways. However, their name is still remembered: firstly by a chapel and vault in St Mary's Church, secondly by a village charity, Mrs. M. D. Dunn's Kintbury Charity, and thirdly by the largest modern housing development in the village which is named Dunn Crescent. This last commemorates not just the Dunn family name, but the work of the last head of family to live in the village, William Hew Dunn.

The Chapel and Vault

The Lady Chapel in the south transept of St Mary's was rebuilt in the later years of the last century with the support of the Dunn family. The three stained glass windows and seven of the memorial plaques are dedicated to various family members.

The Dunn family vault is located to the right of the church's main doorway, and is marked by simple crosses bearing the initials and dates of death of the various Dunn family members. Of particular interest, is the wooden cross (W.D. 1863) of Maj. Gen. William Dunn, who inherited the Inglewood estate from his brother, Thomas, who had bought Inglewood in 1829. Maj. Gen. Dunn wished his grave to be marked as a soldier with a wooden cross. Consequently this has had to be renewed several times by the family, while the other stone crosses have stood the test of time.

Mrs. M. D. Dunn's Kintbury Charity

Mrs. Margaret Duncan Dunn was the widow of Maj. Gen. William Dunn and the mother of seven children. She was the daughter of William Williams Brown, the owner of Wallingtons, and upon her father's death inherited this property, so that from 1850 onwards both the Inglewood and Wallingtons estates were in the ownership of the Dunn family.

Mrs. Dunn was somewhat younger than her husband, and was to remain a widow from his death in 1863 until she died in 1890. However, throughout her life she was a very active lady who, apart from bringing up her large family, thought deeply about the community around her. In the later years of the last century she paid for public baths and wash houses to be built in the High Street at a cost of £4,000. When these facilities were not adequately used Mrs. Dunn had the establishment converted to a laundry which would give employment to the women of the village. This was successful and the 1891 census shows that it employed 11 women and girls, managed by a resident supervisor.

When Mrs. Dunn died in 1890, she left instructions in her will for the establishment of a trust fund to be used for grants for young men and women in Kintbury who were taking up apprenticeships and needed money for tools and clothes for their various trades. When the laundry closed early this century, the sale of this was added to the trust fund, which continues to this day.

In 1863 the Inglewood estate included Templeton, Totterdon House in Inkpen, farms and cottages at Inlease, Broadlands, Sanham Green and Avington, Wallingtons and Balsdon, Hungerford Park, Standen Manor and parts of Bagshot just south of Hungerford.

William Hew Dunn

Willie, as he was known in the family, was the eldest son of William and Margaret Duncan Dunn. He was only 21 when his father died and from that time onwards ran the estate. He married shortly afterwards and lived with his young family at various times at Elcot Park, Standen and Templeton, and following his mother's death at Wallingtons.

William Hew Dunn.

He was Deputy Lieutenant for Berkshire and then High Sheriff in 1874; Captain of the Hungerford Troop of the Royal Berks Yeomanry; M.F.H. of the Craven Hunt on three separate occasions; and Chairman of the Berkshire County Council. Chairman of Kintbury Parish Council from its inception until shortly before his death, he was an active farmer, breeding horses and cattle, a magistrate and particularly active in politics. He died in 1911 aged 69 following a breakdown in health.

William Hew Dunn's funeral following his death on the 26th May 1911 must have been the most impressive that Kintbury has ever witnessed. A contemporary account records that Willie's coffin of unvarnished oak was placed upon a farm wagon, harnessed by four horses which he himself had bred. In the driver's seat was Joseph Hughes, an octogenarian carter who had been in the service of the family for 63 years. At the head of each horse was one of the estate workers. Behind the wagon came a carriage with the sorrowing widow and her daughter. Folllowing immediately behind on foot were the three sons and three surviving brothers of Mr. Dunn, the household servants and a long line of mourners including most of the villagers of Kintbury.

This procession went from Wallingtons to St Mary's Church. In the village, shops were closed and blinds drawn at every house. Church Street was lined with spectators including the schoolchildren. Six clergy led by the Bishop of Oxford conducted the service within the church, and the bishop read the committal as the coffin was lowered into the vault beside the church door.

After Willie's death the Dunn family were not to play a significant part in the life of Kintbury. Willie had already sold the Inglewood estate to Mr. Humphrey Walmesley in 1893 together with Hungerford Park. His widow, Agnes, sold Wallingtons in 1912 to Arthur Stuart Gladstone (grandnephew of W.E. Gladstone, the Victorian Prime Minister) and moved to Titcomb Manor where she died in 1919. Titcomb was inherited by their eldest son, W. S. Dunn, known as Billy, who lived there with his sister, Mina until he moved to Majorca in 1933, Mina remaining there until she died in 1938.

Willie's younger brother, Duncan, inherited Standen Manor. After commanding the Hampshire Regiment in Burma, he married and moved into Standen where his two eldest children Tom and Honor were born. Tom was later killed in 1914 and is commemorated not only in the Dunn chapel, but also on the war memorial.

Major Piers Dunn is the great-grandson of Maj. Gen. William Dunn, and Mrs. Margaret Duncan Dunn.

Fires and Firemen

by Heather Turner

Elsewhere we have mentioned problems at the beginning of the century with Kintbury's ancient fire engine. These were never resolved and we have no record of an active local service until we come to the Second World War and the period just after. It was round about 1946 that Percy Morris, who had seen active service in the National Auxiliary Fire Service, fighting fires in the Southampton Blitz and elsewhere, approached the Parish Council for support in setting up a voluntary service in Kintbury. The Council debated this on and off for some time before giving the idea its blessing; and so Kintbury was allocated a fire pump trailer. Then came the problem of finding a vehicle which could always be readily available to tow it and of course somewhere to keep it! This was eventually resolved by Kintbury Garage coming to the rescue with car, driver and storage. Further difficulties emerged in not having a sufficient length of hose, but this was overcome and the Kintbury Service got under way. Percy Morris was First Officer and his Second-in-Command was Arthur Head who had also seen service fighting fires in Liverpool, Portsmouth and other places in the war.

The Voluntary Firefighters were summoned by a portable hooter which was in the charge of Mrs. Ethel Druce at the garage. On receiving an emergency call she would take the hooter, which was kept in the office, out into the yard and crank it up by hand. She said that it produced "the most awful din!" The volunteers were required to undertake regular practice drills and had to maintain their numbers at not less than 12. Unfortunately, the service was disbanded after just a few years but they were proud of their achievement of being 'first on the scene' when fire broke out at Notrees (the original house) when alterations were being carried out to turn it into a home for the elderly.

Kintbury has been fortunate in not having many serious fires during the century. Those remembered include a fire at Inglewood House in 1912, the burning down of Star Cottages at Blandys Hill, followed by two days later a serious fire at Kintbury Garage round about 1926. After the Second World War a cottage was destroyed in Newbury Street and also one at Wawcott. No-one was hurt in any of these blazes.

Living at Osmington in the 20s and 30s

by Angela Stansfeld

The Rennie family came to Osmington House in 1921. My father was a retired Brigadier General. He had a long military career both in the Boer War and First World War. He had served on the Western Front throughout the entire war, returning only on leave. He must have been one of only a handful who survived the entire war fighting in the trenches. He lost practically all his friends. He won the DSO in the Boer War and was mentioned in Despatches seven times in the Great War. My mother ran the household at Osmington and there were three of us girls – my sisters Winifred and Evelyn, and me. Though others may have considered us well off, we lived quite modestly. Despite this we were able to employ four indoor staff and a gardener. We provided work for five people at a time when jobs were not easy to find. The staff were a cook-general, parlourmaid, housemaid and another maid whose particular job was to look after my sisters and me.

During most of my childhood I did not go out to school but had a governess who came daily from Newbury. Later I did go to school for about two years but after that I did not train for any sort of career, nor did my sisters. This was the decision of our parents. Father explained to us that it was not right for us to have jobs as we would be taking away work from others whose need was greater. So we found ourselves leading what some might consider a rather idle life. Nevertheless we had no difficulty in filling our days. Our upbringing was fairly disciplined. We were always expected to be at meals on time, which included breakfast! We were told it was unfair on our staff not to be. We were never allowed to read in the mornings if we were at home – but we could write letters – and there were plenty of these to send – 'thank-you' letters for invitations – before and after the event, and correspondence with relatives and friends. It was a great letter-writing era – telephones were not all that common and we girls were not allowed to use ours anyway.

So how did we occupy ourselves? In the early days I had a garden which I was expected to look after. In summer there were many tennis parties. Most of the large houses locally had courts, as we did at Osmington. I remember particularly the Thomas's at Elcot Park. They had three sons and five courts, so that was quite a popular place to go! We went swimming a lot, not in private pools – there weren't many of these – but in the canal and local rivers. We had a couple of favourite spots where the water was beautifully clear and no weeds. In winter there was hunting – usually twice a week. We would go to the meet by car and our groom would collect and bring the horses. However when the Hunt was over we were expected to ride the horses home ourselves. If the meet happened to be somewhere like the Lambourn area this was quite a ride – and a very long day!

I'm sure winters were colder then and we certainly had more ice and snow. Tobogganing was a regular activity – and another treat was skating on the canal. Favourite place was between Brunsdon Lock and the railway bridge towards Hungerford. Here the water froze solidly at times and we would set off along the towpath with our folding ladder. This was in case we fell in – but we never did! As children we were taught to play Bridge, which my father described as an essential skill and one which would prove extremely useful to us as a social activity in later life. "You will have a miserable old age if you don't play Bridge," he would say.

In the evenings there were many parties and dances at local houses like Stargroves, Highclere Castle, Elcot and Hungerford Park. The latter was well known for its Firework parties thrown at any excuse like celebrations of family birthdays and similar occasions.

The staff had their parties too. Usually these were in the form of Annual Balls. They certainly took place at Stargroves and Highclere, and there were very large parties with staff from many nearby houses invited.

Living conditions at Osmington were fairly spartan. It was ice cold in winter as there was no central heating. We just had an open fire in our drawing room and would huddle around this to keep warm. Our electricity was supplied in the early days by Mr. Phillips from his Electric Lighting Works in the village. Water was not laid on as there was no mains supply. Like other houses we had a well and water from here was pumped up by hand to a tank in the roof. It took three-quarters of an hour each day to do this job and it was our gardener who did this! I felt very sorry for him sometimes. This water supplied our indoor needs including our one family bathroom. Our staff had their bath too – but I am afraid it was of the old 'hip' variety serviced with cans of water!

We had no refrigerator, neither did most houses. This did not matter too much as all local shops delivered daily and there were regular calls from shops further afield in Hungerford and Newbury.

As a family we were involved a little in village life. My mother delivered the Parish magazine and belonged to the Women's Institute. I joined the Girl Guides when the Kintbury troop started up in 1926. My father had his

Osmington House.

interests too, especially the British Legion. It was fairly common for him to walk along the canal to Newbury, meet his friends for Bridge and then catch the train back to Kintbury, and he was still doing this into his seventies. When war threatened in the 1930s he was ready to serve his country again. He was all packed up and ready to go, but the anticipated call-up did not materialise when the Czechoslovakian crisis ended with Neville Chamberlain's visit to Munich. His chance came not long after though when, after the outbreak of the Second World War, he commanded the Kintbury Platoon of the Home Guard.

I remember the 20s and 30s as a tranquil time in Kintbury when life was lived at a much more leisurely pace than today. Particular incidents are not so easy to recall but I do remember the General Strike of 1926. It was all hands to the pump then and my uncle, John Rennie, stood in as a train driver and distinguished himself by getting stuck on Kintbury level crossing!

I was kept well informed of the progress of the strike by a friend in London who wrote almost daily about events in the capital. Incidentally at that time the cheap day fare to London was only 7/6d (about 35p).

Another special memory for me of those inter-war years was my Presentation at Court in 1930. This was to King George V and all his sons, the Prince of Wales (later the Duke of Windsor) and the Dukes of York, Gloucester and Kent were there on that day.

I married in 1939 and left Kintbury but returned in the 50s. It was at about this time that our family home, Osmington House was sold for less than £5000 – a figure that seems hardly possible today. With my husband, Hamer, and son Anthony, we settled into 'Tuttles'. Anthony with his wife Nicky and their daughter live in the house now and I live in the cottage, nicely converted from a previous carpenter's shop. I still play tennis and greatly enjoy my Bridge, sometimes playing three or four times a week with my friends. My father was right!

In conclusion, the Rennie family's connection with Kintbury goes back a long way for it was my Great Great Grandfather, the celebrated Engineer, John Rennie, who was responsible for the construction of the Kennet and Avon Canal.

Inglewood, Wallingtons and The De La Salle Brothers

by Sybil Flinn

Catholicism gained a meeting place in Kintbury when Mr. Humphrey Jeffreys Walmsley bought the Inglewood Estate from Mr. Huw Dunn in 1893. The Walmsleys were an old Lancashire Catholic family who decided to move south when their ancestral home was surrounded and indeed, undermined, by the spread of industry in Lancashire. The Walmsleys were very devout Catholics and had their family chapel dismantled, brought to Inglewood and re-erected. Local Kintbury Catholics who had formerly to travel to Newbury or Marlborough for worship, were invited to the Walmsley chapel, which was large enough for about 150 people.

In 1919 Humphrey Walmsley died and Inglewood passed to his son, Col. Charles Walmsley, and he decided in 1928 to put the estate up for auction in 47 lots, including other properties such as Hungerford Park House (which was sold to the Turners). Inglewood itself, a very large house – 28 bed and dressing rooms, but only 3 bathrooms and 5 wc's – failed to sell.

Before a second auction could be arranged, which may well have resulted in the house being demolished and its grounds divided for building plots, the property was brought to the notice of the De la Salle Congregation in the U.K., a Catholic order, who were looking for a property to serve as a college for boys, who would eventually enter the brothers' teaching order. The Lasallians' representative, Brother Benedict, came to see Inglewood House and met Col. Walmsley, who was delighted with the thought that the property would continue in Catholic hands. A deal was struck and Inglewood House with approximately 50 acres of grounds was sold to the De la Salle Order for £7,000 in November 1928.

This was the beginning of the Lasallians stay in Kintbury which continues to this day. Inglewood House was re-named St. John's College. At the commencement, 40 boys from 13 upwards and 24 young novices were housed as well as senior staff. Gradually these numbers would grow to between 80 and 100 in total. The new arrivals lived to a strict regime and, to a great extent, were a very self-contained community. The village, however, supplied some of their needs: bread came from Rolfe's bakery, Seymour Harrod was assistant gardener, and Cecil Bailey and Tom Pike were employed as cooks. The scholars played football in winter and cricket in summer within the grounds of the house, and swam in the canal during the summer months.

During the war years, St. John's College continued its educational role, but numbers were slightly increased by brothers who had fled occupied France and the Channel Islands. Part of the grounds were dug up for growing more vegetables, and Italian prisoners of war, who were at a local camp, came to Inglewood to worship.

In 1945, Wallingtons, which is adjacent to Inglewood, was put up for sale. Mr. Arthur Steuart Gladstone, who had lived at Wallingtons since 1912 died in 1940, and the house had been bought shortly after his death by Edwards Bros., owners of the sawmills at Inkpen, presumably for the extensive woodlands. However, in 1945, the house was again put on the market and was bought by the Lasallians for £13,500 to provide a separate school for the Junior boys (13 to 16-18 years old), who moved in, leaving Inglewood for the Novices and those doing their professional training. Wallingtons became St. Cassians for the Lasallians.

It could not have been foreseen that this increase in accommodation at Kintbury would eventually prove unwanted. In the post-war years the numbers of young men (and women, too) seeking to enter a religious order and take vows of poverty, chastity and obedience declined greatly. In 1971 numbers at Inglewood had fallen below thirty and the community was forced to consider what was best to accommodate the Order's scholars in the future. The decision to vacate Inglewood, which was proving a very expensive old house to maintain, was made. The house was advertised for sale in October 1971, but attracted only one firm offer of £50,000, which was accepted. Inglewood now entered the third phase of its existence, as the new owners totally refurbished the property to create the Health Hydro, which it is today.

One very poignant reminder of the Lasallians period at Inglewood remains. There is a small cemetery at the rear of the house where the Brothers who died during the Order's ownership are buried. The graves are tended by their present-day brethren at Wallingtons.

Meanwhile at Wallingtons, now St. Cassians, the house continued as a school for junior boys until the early 1970s when a change of use was decided by the De la Salle Order. St. Cassians would become a Retreat Centre, which would complement the programme of Religious Education in the Catholic schools, and 84 of these use the Centre.

The Retreat Centre opened in 1975. It is run by a permanent team of De la Salle Brothers, and two Sisters, while six or seven young volunteers stay for one year.

Throughout the year individual school groups of 10 to 12 boys and girls share their experience with similar groups from other schools, drawn from all parts of the country. There are also Family Groups covering every age, and Advent and Lent retreats for adults, and a Kintbury Churches Together Group comes every year. St. Cassians is no longer the remote part of the Kintbury community which St. John's College was. To those who come, and thousands do every year, Kintbury is a place to remember, perhaps return to joyfully in the years to come.

St. Cassians Centre team 1998–99: De la Salle brothers, Dominican sisters and volunteers.

(Below)
Wallingtons –
St. Cassians Centre.

Kintbury Methodism

by Rev. Colin Scarrett

Methodism came to Kintbury in the early 19th century. This new denomination became established in the 18th century from the Nonconformist tradition. Nonconformists were 'Dissenters' who failed to comply with the Act of Uniformity in 1662 and were ejected out of the Church of England. In the late 17th century the Toleration Act was passed which allowed most Nonconformists to have their own places of worship 'so long as they met with doors unlocked and notified the bishop of their existence'.

A clergyman asked John Wesley "In what points to you differ from the Church of England?" He answered, "To the best of my knowledge in none". Wesley was then asked, "In what points then, do you differ from other clergy of the Church of England?" He answered, "In none from that part of the clergy who adhere to the doctrine of the church".

However by 1739 John Wesley found himself excluded from almost all Anglican pulpits in London. This was because he preached in the open air wherever there was an audience. Open air preaching was illegal for any clergyman outside his own parish.

The conditions of the day made Wesley's preaching very relevant. There was a constant fear of death from diseases like typhoid, smallpox, typhus and dysentery. Violence and drunkenness was common in an age when the judicial system imposed very harsh punishments for really quite minor offences. Thefts of small sums of money were punishable by hanging. Transportation was a frequent sentence. John Wesley told people that God loved them all and wanted them saved.

The Wesleyan Church in Inkpen Road was built around 1824 and was extended in 1834 because the congregation became too large for it. The Zion Church was opened in October 1853 in the High Street. However both of these Methodist Churches had roots before this time, originally meeting in people's homes and even in a carthouse. Unrest over southern England in 1830 – protesting over the Enclosure Act, which deprived the farm labourers from using the common land – developed into the Kintbury Riots, which brought Government forces from London to quell the 'uprising'. Wesley had condemned the poverty of the people in his time and Methodism was a natural spiritual home for people struggling under difficult conditions.

Both Methodist Churches attracted large numbers of people to worship in non-conformist style and had thriving Sunday Schools for the local children. The Zion Church closed and is now a private house. The Methodist Church in Inkpen Road was sold in 1994 and the church moved into the adjoining Church Hall.

The divisions of the past are now thankfully gone and there is a strong worshipping community in Kintbury across all denominations.

Kintbury Methodist Church,
Inkpen Road.

The Story of My Life on Leaving School

by Elsie Turfrey

On leaving school at the age of 14 in 1924, I went into domestic service to the late Arthur William Edwards, then vicar of Kintbury, on a temporary basis to cover staff holidays. Quite a few in those days as the Edwards' kept a cook, parlourmaid, nurse and housemaid for their family of eight children in the large vicarage at the bottom of Church Street.

My first permanent job was with the Mackworth family at Green Gates on the Inkpen Road, serving there for ten years, after which I left to be cook to the late Dr. Edmund Hemsted. Dr. Hemsted was at that time the senior village GP and his home was the original 'No Trees' off the High Street. After Dr. Hemsted's death, 'No Trees' became a home for the elderly – that being his wish, and was later demolished and the present sheltered housing and care complex built in its place. However, by that time I had already left Dr. Hemstead's employment as both my parents were ill and they needed me at home. There I stayed for two years, when first my father passed away, soon followed by my mother. My sister and two brothers were already married, so I was left to carry on the home on my own at No. 9 High Street. It was the year 1945.

After taking a short break, I prepared myself to get back into work. Feeling I wanted a change from domestic duties, I decided to take an outdoor occupation on seeing an advert for 'Dairy Work' in the village shop. I applied and was taken on by Messrs. Killick and Bevan, farming partners, who lived in adjoining houses at Layland's Green. So there I was about to start a new adventure.

My first duties were assisting Mr. Killick with milk delivery to Wallingtons, which was done by horse and cart, the milk in an old-fashioned milk churn was measured out as needed by the customer. Not long after we changed to a motorised vehicle, which enabled us to enlarge our delivery area around the village. Mr. Killick did the driving. After the first week, I was beginning to enjoy my new venture, also, it was suggested by the family that I might take charge of the takings. I soon came to terms with my responsibilities, making sure of giving the right change etc. When the rounds were finished, my help was needed in the dairy, cooling and bottling the milk for the next day, which I found very interesting. Mr. Bevan with his farmhand, Joe Thorn, did the milking by hand – they had a very nice Jersey herd. Mrs. Bevan did the accounts and

rounds books, whilst their niece, Carrie, who made her home with them, also gave a hand.

As time passed, Mr. Killick's health failed, so Carrie took his place, as driver, on the rounds with me. It was not long after that Mr. Killick passed away, which meant the whole burden fell on the Bevan family. In due course, agewise, it became too much for them to carry on, so they decided to sell the business. I was very sorry, because I found them very nice to work for. Mr. Trice of Woolton Hill bought the milk business and the farmhand, Joe Thorn, and myself carried on for him.

This change meant more travelling. We both cycled to Woolton Hill early each morning to collect the milk van and then start on the round back to Kintbury. Then we returned to Woolton Hill to do our books, and finally cycle home to Kintbury. This really kept us fit! But alas, after about two years, Mr. Trice decided he had had enough of milk distribution, and the business was sold to Heatherwold Dairy in Newbury.

This being our second move, our thoughts were, are we here to stay or would we be upended again. Yes! True enough, after a short while we learned that we were being transferred to Hungerford, to be taken over by Rectory Farm Dairy at 5a High Street. Joe, as driver, who had been with me through all these moves, decided that he had had enough and went off to work elsewhere. That left me on my own to carry on doing the village.

That was the start of my being issued with a hand-driven but electrically propelled truck. Though walking with the truck, I still had to take a driving test and my subsequent licence is in my possession to this day. The firm managed to rent a garage in Kintbury at the top end of High Street for this vehicle, where a charger had to be installed for me to change the batteries overnight ready for the next day. The Milk – some 600 pints in crates was brought out from Hungerford and loaded on to the hand cart, even on the roof.

My new truck caused great interest in the village, as I walked my rounds, driving the truck and giving the correct road signals! As the years passed, so the village grew, many more houses being built and soon occupied, meant many more deliveries to make. But I enjoyed it all, and the customers were very nice to me – plenty of cups of tea etc., and excellent tips at Christmas. Weather conditions through the years varied enormously but you had to take this in your stride. So that was the second chapter of my working life lasting 25 years until I retired at pensionable age. It is all very nice to look back on.

Editor's note:
Elsie retired from her milk round in 1970, but she has been far from idle since. After a short spell at home, she was asked by Mr. and Mrs. Jim Sandiford if she could help them in their newsagents on the corner of High Street and Inkpen Road, sorting out the newspapers for the delivery rounds. Once more Elsie found herself working from 5 to 9am. She worked in this way for years and currently still arrives at the Corner Stores to collect and deliver the daily papers for the residents and tenants at No Trees.

In 1983 the Rev. Martin Gillham was appointed Vicar of St. Mary's and shortly afterwards asked Elsie if she would serve as Verger. This role, Elsie was very pleased to undertake, as her father had been a Churchwarden and her brother, John, Verger in earlier years. Elsie was Verger until 1990 when she retired from that appointment. But once more, not for long, for when the Rev. Debby Plummer was appointed, she asked Elsie if she would assist her in readying the church for weddings, funerals and communions – a role which she happily undertakes to date.

Serving the Customer

Eileen Thatcher remembers

Born at Hamstead Marshall, where three generations of the Punter family had a building and decorating business, Eileen Thatcher went to school in Newbury. On leaving school Eileen was offered a job as an assistant in Chisletts Stores in Kintbury in 1928 and started work on August Bank Holiday Saturday at 2/6d a week (half-a-crown as it was known then, or 12½p today). Not a bad wage for a beginner at that time. She continued to live at home and cycled from Hamstead Marshall, going back to Hamstead for her lunch hour. The hours were long: 8 to 6 Monday to Wednesday, half day Thursday, then 8 to 7 Friday and 8 to 8 Saturday! Standing at the counter the whole time, the first days on the job seemed endless and exhausting.

Chisletts, which occupied the premises on the corner of Church Street and High Street, now the Corner Stores and Post Office, was owned and run by Mr. and Mrs. Chislett. There were two entrances and the premises were divided into a grocer's shop and a drapers. The name Chisletts can be still be seen in the floor of the present shop entrance. There was also a bakery in the buildings at the rear. Nearly all the produce sold at that time was bought in bulk and then weighed and wrapped for the customer – butter, lard, tea, dried fruit, rice, biscuits, bacon, cheese were just some of the items which were measured out. Much of this produce carried brand names still familiar – Typhoo Tea, Brooke Bond, Lyons, McVities, Peek Freans. The shop packaging was a square of paper used to wrap each item – "Imagine me during my first days, struggling to wrap 8ozs of rice without spilling any", says Eileen with feeling. Biscuits came in large square 7lb tins, the broken ones being sold off at a cheaper price. Dried fruit arrived in heavy 28lb boxes. There was no refrigeration – the shop had electric light only supplied by a water driven generator at Kintbury Mill – and the perishable food was stored in the coolness of the cellar, and brought up to the shop in smaller quantities as needed and then kept on a marble slab. The assistants served each customer with their individual requirements, wrote and added up the bills and put the money in a cash drawer.

Chisletts, although not the only grocers in Kintbury, was a busy place. In addition to customers coming to the shop, there were many account customers who ordered for home delivery, and a thriving bread round serving a wide area – Hoe Benham, Stockcross, Inkpen, Wickham and as far as Lambourn. Transport, apart from local carriers and the railway, was non-existent in those early inter-war days and many people walked miles to and from their homes, and carried back large bags with their weekly shop. Mrs. Thatcher remembers especially old Mrs. Tilley who came from Titcomb and another customer who walked from Combe every Saturday.

Over the years, Eileen took on more responsibilities in the business. Although she worked hard, she enjoyed the job getting to know the customers and their requirements; it was Eileen says "all so personal". When World War II started in 1939 came rationing and another chore for the shopkeeper. Everyone had a ration book divided into pages of little coupons, which had to be clipped out by the shopkeeper for sugar, tea, butter and other essential items.

These little coupons, smaller than postage stamps, had to be counted up and returned to the 'Ministry' offices in Newbury to authorise future bulk orders. There was no time during the day, so Eileen took them home on Saturday night and counted there!

Eileen Thatcher worked for Chisletts until 1946. She had married her childhood sweetheart, Pete, in 1941, and continued to work at the shop while Pete was in the Army, spending four years (without leave) in Burma. When Pete came home in February 1946 they had a son, Richard, and their first home in Harold Road and the family took priority – but not for long. In a few years a new chapter serving the public began.

When Pete Thatcher returned from the war, he resumed his trade as a butcher with Dennis Hunt at his business now in Church Street. Following the death of Mr. Hunt, Pete Thatcher took over the business and later bought the premises, which then became Thatchers.

Pete Thatcher did not only sell meat, he raised and slaughtered his own animals – cattle and pigs – only lamb being bought in. The animals were kept at a smallholding at Cullamores and driven down to Thatchers yard, behind the shop, where they were humanely slaughtered. Three to four beef cattle and some six to eight pigs were needed to stock the shop each week. Later, in the 50s new regulations were introduced, making it obligatory for slaughtering to be done in licensed abattoirs, so Thatchers' pigs and beef went to Newbury on Monday morning and their carcasses were collected later in the day.

During the years when the Thatchers ran their business, the British public enjoyed their meat – no BSE problems or vegetarian movement to depress the trade. By rearing and stocking top-quality produce and perfecting a prize-winning sausage recipe, Pete Thatcher expanded the business. Eileen was a very able partner, filling in on delivery rounds, serving in the shop, or making sausages – every day was busy.

In the post-war years Thatchers became the only butcher in Kintbury, serving a wide area from Highclere to Lambourn, with the famous sausages in demand to fill orders from the Isle of Skye, France and Switzerland. Christmas was a nightmare with hundreds of turkeys to be plucked and dressed.

In December 1985 Pete and Eileen Thatcher felt the time had come to retire, the business and premises were sold and they moved to a bungalow in Hungerford. Thatchers name was retained by the new owners and the premises, excluding the shop itself, converted into various units – an estate agent's office, a tea room and several small shops in the old yard, although small signs of the original use still remain. But Eileen, now alone following Pete's death in 1987 looks back with fond memories of those many years serving the customers.

Kintbury in Wartime

by Heather Turner

Little is recorded about the wars which took place early in this century. We do have the *Newbury Weekly News* report that Mr. Argyle, headmaster of St. Mary's School, organised the children to celebrate and go round the streets spreading the news of the relief of Ladysmith in the Boer War. When we come to the 1914–1918 War it seems that village life carried on much as usual. The horrors of trench warfare across the Channel were remote without the radio and T.V. cover of today, excepting that is for those families in Kintbury who lost loved ones – and there were 53 local men who were killed in action in that war – so it was obviously a time of great grief for many in our closely-knit community of those days.

War came nearer when Barton Court, home then of Lord Burnham, became a convalescent home for wounded soldiers and local people helped out there including children from St. Mary's School. Whilst news of what happened in the war years is scarce, the celebration of the peace is well recorded. The Parish Council set up a committee of local people to organise 'Peace Teas'. These were to be paid for by public subscription. A tea for the children was arranged for Thursday, 17th July 1919 and they were given time off from school to attend. They also received a 'Peace Mug'. On the following Saturday, 19th July, there was a 'Free Tea' for returned soldiers (and 'others' if there was room). Fireworks and sports were to be included. These events took place at Wallingtons, the home of Mr. A. S. Gladstone, who did so much for Kintbury during the time he lived here.

So we come to 1939 and the Second World War. Those of us alive then no doubt remember just where we were when war was declared on 3rd September that year, when a strange feeling of fear and uncertainty came over us. Schools closed, the entertainments stopped and the order came that no church bells must be rung for the duration – unless our country was invaded when they would ring out to warn us. After a few days we all realised that life had to go on, the schools reopened and everyone turned their attention to 'doing their bit' for the war effort.

The 'Call Up' came and all young men of 18 and over were required to join the forces unless in a 'reserved occupation'. As time went on older men were called up too and so the village was short of menfolk – but not for long. As the war progressed, troops moved in all around us. Huts appeared in the woodlands at Barton Court, Hamstead Marshall and other places. First it was British troops, but later Americans too. Those at Barton Court were part of a Searchlight Repair Battery and so at night the sky would be lit up with searchlights scanning the heavens. Quite eerie and somewhat frightening we children found it.

On the 'home front' much was happening. Air Raid Wardens were recruited and we had our own detachment of the Observer Corps who nightly manned a rather ramshackle observation post which was built in the area where The Pentlands is now. Their job was to observe and report on enemy aircraft movements.

The ladies were involved too. Every woman who did not have young children was expected to help the war effort by joining the women's forces, doing essential factory work or was recruited into the Land Army, nursing or one of the auxiliary services. Local detachments of the Red Cross and St. John Ambulance Brigade recruited many Kintbury women and Lady Spickernel, much respected and admired locally, was in charge. A huge spirit of comradeship grew up and everyone was willing to make their particular contribution. Even those working full time in shops and offices in Newbury did their extra bit. Christine Hall, now a retired Woolworth's supervisor, was expected on a rota basis to spend nights 'fire-watching' on the first floor above the shop and yet turn up for duty the next day and there were many more like her. The great fear was the dropping of incendiary bombs. The Coronation Hall became the focal point for our civilian wartime activities. Gas masks were issued from there, so were ration books. The billeting officers who were responsible for finding homes for evacuees operated from there. Emergency supplies were stored there. For a time it was manned 24 hours a day with the Red Cross sharing this duty with the Air Raid Wardens. Nevertheless the hall, or parts of it, remained available for social occasions and these were important as we all had to keep our spirits up. Concerts were held there when those with talent – and there were quite a few – acted out humorous sketches, sang songs, recited poems and told funny stories, all in aid of the war effort and the audience paid for their seats with War Savings Stamps. There was no formal drama group in the village then but even so acting and singing performances were of a high standard. Later, with the war well under way, our hall throbbed to the music of many bands, often supplied by troops stationed nearby, as local girls and they danced the night away. These lighter moments were very necessary to counteract the long weary years of war and the efforts and sacrifices made by so many.

Food rationing came early in the war to be followed by clothes rationing. Both stayed for many years even after peace was declared because of continuing shortages. Petrol was rationed too and most cars were ordered off the roads. This was probably as well since all signposts were removed and vehicle lights had to be dimmed to the extent that it was almost impossible to see where you were going. Also the petrol pumps at Kintbury Garage were taken over by the military, so no local fuel. Only prescribed 'essential' vehicles were allowed.

'Enterprise' was the name of the game then, nobly displayed by our Women's Institute who started up a 'jam factory' in the outbuildings at Inglewood Lodge. Local fruits in season were 'jammed' and the schoolchildren did their bit by picking pounds and pounds of blackberries, having been given time off from school to do this. Children, through their Scout, Cub, Guide and Brownie Packs collected paper and foil for 'salvage'. As a Brownie I remember special 'knitting evenings' organised by Miss Sybil Dopson our 'Brown Owl' at her home 'Fairview' in Inkpen Road. We made 'mittens for the troops'. Since for most of us our knitting skills were just above zero on a nought to ten scale I've often wondered what happened to our finished products – nobody ever told us!

invading troops and tanks. So the army, with considerable help from civilian building contractors, worked long hours building pillboxes along the canal. At places in the Kintbury area transport of materials would have been difficult and the canal would have been used to move these, as would the railway. In Kintbury Parish there were nine pillboxes, sited at Mill Lane, The Avenue and along the length of the canal, mostly near bridges and locks. Five were demolished at various times after the War, including one in Mill Lane which was blown up with near-disastrous results. So four were left and you will come across them in your canal walks. The pillbox which still remains on Hungerford Common was rather different to the rest and was designed for a two pound anti-tank gun, whereas most of the others were meant for machine guns which could

A pillbox on the canal.

Then there was a Red Cross Working Party who knitted and sewed their way through the war, making a total of 4,001 garments which included special orders for pyjamas for the Royal Artillery, hessian aprons for the A.T.S. (What were they for?), socks and gloves for our P.O.Ws and baby clothes to be sent to liberated countries.

Whilst all this was going on, in the very early days of the War, there was a real threat of invasion by the Germans and so in 1940 the Government Home Defence Department decided that the Kennet and Avon Canal, for most of its length, would be an inland defence line against

provide crossfire, covering long stretches of the canal. On the brick-built bridges, square concrete blocks about nine inches across were let into the road or grass track and they are still there. These could be removed and piles or R.S.Js could be lowered about two feet into the holes to prevent tanks crossing. The bridge over the canal by the Old Vicarage also had a number of heavy round concrete blocks stored alongside the bridge which were also designed to stop tanks. These were removed some time after the war.

As a further defence against invasion the Local

Defence Volunteers were formed, later to be known as the Home Guard. Kintbury had its own detachment formed from older men, those in reserved occupations and young men awaiting call-up. They were under the control of Brigadier General Rennie and they took their role very seriously. There were 'warfare practices' at weekends with pitched battles against Hungerford Home Guard and sometimes the Regular Army. Very strange things happened in these battles sometimes. 'H.Q.' was an old shepherd's hut located near 'The Firs' on Blandys Hill – a good vantage point as it looked down over all the village. At one time this was manned nightly on a rota basis by two members of the Home Guard. Later when threat of invasion receded, manning took place only when the air raid siren (mounted on top of Hungerford Police Station) sounded. Peter Lambourn, who lived here then, and was a young Home Guard, was 'knocker-up' and it was his job to cycle round in the dark (no lights) calling the men out for duty – which was to look out for fire bombs.

On the Hungerford Road just below Inglewood Cottage where we lived at the beginning of the war, a 'defence barrier' was placed. This was a rather rickety pole fixed on a pivot at one end and with a large wheel at the other and covered in coils of barbed wire. The idea was that if there was an invasion scare, this could be wheeled across the road to stop the enemy's advance. Stored in a shed at the bottom of our garden and near this barrier were bottles containing a curious liquid (petrol?) which we children were told not to touch. These bottles could be hurled by the Home Guard at an approaching enemy, presumably from behind this barricade! There are some of us who know that the T.V. series 'Dad's Army' is based on fact, not fiction!

Being a quiet country area, though we prepared for bombs, we didn't really expect them to fall here. However, on the night of 3rd September 1941, they did! Three of them – at Home Farm, at the top of Newbury Street, and near to Laylands Green. No-one was hurt but slight damage was done to a row of houses above and to the north of Newbury Street. This was a minor incident compared to the devastation suffered in many places but the noise of those explosions terrified many of us that night.

Back on the Home Front everyone was being urged to 'Dig for Victory'. Front lawns of some houses were dug up and spuds and other crops grown. Another aid to agriculture came in the form of Italian and German prisoners housed in huts and behind wire opposite Hamstead Holt Farm. These were employed on the land in various places locally. Some dug drainage ditches in the water meadows, worked on farms and some assisted at St.

John's College (now the Health Hydro) where those who were Catholics were allowed to worship.

Responding to a call from the government for scrap metal, the Parish Council organised a collection in Kintbury and this is when many of our village houses lost their railings. Arrangements were made with Charlie Burridge, the garage proprietor, for the metal to be stored there and then it was eventually sold for the sum of £32.

Every so often the government, desperately short of money to continue fighting the War, called for special 'savings' weeks to be held when money was raised through the sale of National Savings Stamps and Certificates. These had names like 'War Weapons' and 'Wings for Victory' weeks. Targets were set for each town and village and everyone beavered away organising events which raised huge sums of money by the standards of those days. All sorts of events were held and those attending paid in savings stamps. They had another spin-off too, as those who went thoroughly enjoyed themselves and there was a much-needed lifting of spirits away from the gloom of the dark days of war.

As time passed it became evident that we were actually winning the war and that peace would soon return. So people relaxed a bit and thoughts turned to how we would celebrate and welcome 'the boys' home from the war. The Women's Institute, Girls' Club and others began raising funds and making plans so that when hostilities did cease there were tremendous celebrations which included street parties, bonfires, military parades and, not least, Thanksgiving Services to express relief that nearly six long weary years of war were over. Two hundred and twenty-five returning servicemen received 'Thank You' certificates from the people of Kintbury, together with a sum of just over £4 shared out from the Celebration Fund.

But there was sadness too because though casualties were not nearly as great as in the First World War, 16 of our men were killed in action and their names, together with those who fell in the 1914–18 War are included in this book.

Details of the canal defences supplied by Denis Turner.

...nbers of Kintbury's Civil Defence Service.
...nt centre: Johnny Killick.

Kintbury's Home Guard platoon.

The British Legion

by Alfred Martyn-Johns

The British Legion movement was formed in May 1921 by bringing together the four then existing national organisations of ex-servicemen, which had come into being as a result of the First World War.

The objectives of the British Legion are first to promote the welfare of serving and ex-servicemen and women, and the widows, children and dependants of those who have served, and to relieve hardship where it exists: and secondly to raise and distribute money for these purposes.

The Kintbury & District Branch of the Royal British Legion was formed in 1931. During the 1914-18 war, Kintbury lost fifty-three men. The names of these men were first recorded on a wooden memorial which was erected in the Square. On Sunday, 30th March 1919, a fine granite memorial was dedicated by the Bishop of Oxford, witnessed by a large crowd of Kintbury people, many of whom had lost members of their family or relatives and neighbours. Kintbury was a very close-knit community. After the Second World War a further sixteen names were added to the Memorial.

A service of remembrance has been held at the Memorial on Armistice Day 11th November, or later on Remembrance Sunday, for the last eighty years. On the formation of the Branch, members of the British Legion headed up a parade of Scouts, Girl Guides, Cubs, Brownies and St John Ambulance accompanied by the Inkpen Band to the War Memorial.

The Kintbury Branch was formed with the express intention of supporting ex-servicemen and their families. Many returning servicemen had sustained various injuries and, unemployment being widespread, it was very often difficult to find and compete for the few available vacancies. The British Legion enabled ex-servicemen to get together and provide funds to help their disabled and needy comrades and maintain the many things they had in common through their past experience.

Soon after the 1939-45 war, the Branch recruited more members as servicemen came home and, with the impetus of this new blood, a large Nissen hut was acquired as a Club House and erected by local members close to the Coronation Hall. The premises consisted of three rooms with a central bar, a dance floor on one side and a billiard table and darts on the other side.

The Club House was very popular and many residents have happy memories of the dances held there, which were also attended by the American servicemen stationed at Membury. The local dance band consisted of Sam Benson with his banjo, George Fennel – violin, George Palmer with his drums and Kitty Palmer on the piano or accordion.

The Club was the venue for an annual Dug-Out Supper. On one occasion a large cabbage was brought along by a local farm worker for a 'Guess the Weight' competition. An American soldier guessed the nearest correct weight of 32lbs. The prize was a bottle of whisky. The second prize was the cabbage itself, won by a local man. The American offered to exchange his whisky for the cabbage! The deal was quickly done and no doubt the American re-raffled the cabbage at his base.

Unfortunately the Nissen hut was to be demolished in 1964, the land being required for housing. The Branch, deprived of its own social centre, appears to have lost some membership for a period. In 1983 the Branch was reformed, quickly raising membership from only twenty to forty-six and later to a remarkable seventy-seven. At this time the Branch Standard was refurbished and regularly paraded throughout the County. The Women's Branch was also revived and their Standard paraded once again. By 1986 the Branch was looking for a suitable Club House. The redundant Chilton Factory Social Club building was purchased, dismantled and put in store pending planning permission being obtained for its erection. Unfortunately planning permission was never given and the stored building had to be disposed of in 1990.

The Kintbury & District Branch of the Royal British Legion continues to help the village community to provide for the relief of ex-Servicemen and their dependants everywhere and to keep alive the memory of the sixty-eight men on the memorial.

Albert Cook (centre), Albert Rose (right).
Can you identify the third man?

In Memory of those Kintbury Men who gave their lives on Active Service
1914-1918

Sidney Pearce	Sidney Dopson	Francis Burton	Albert Mills	Sidney Wyman
Frederick Hamblin	Arthur Edwards	Percy Cooper	John Alder	Arthur Bradley
Ernest Talbot	Robert Tuttle	Henry Sturgess	Frederick Martin	Thomas Fidler
James Compton	William Martin	George Smart	William Alder	Thomas Dunn
George Smoker	Thomas Alexander	Edward Edwards	William Hayward	Ernest Pinchin
Harry Hobday	Charles White	Francis Martin	William Gilbert	William White
Ernest Herbert	William Chislett	John King	Charles Morris	Harry Thorpe
Edward Little	Charles King	Edwin Wilde	Sidney Holmes	Edward Hughes
Frank Hobday	William Hessey	William Burton	John Cook	Frederick Litten
Frank Edwards	Frederick Little	Edward Drew	Henry Braxton	
John Budd	Walter Read	Leonard Stroud	Richard Sutton	

1939-1945

Herbert Head	Desmond Cook	James Gillman
Stanley Hunt	Christopher Mackworth	Kenneth Thorne
Sidney Abraham	Richard Cook	Frederick Harris
Howard Kent	William Dance	Paul Wallace
Stanley Bailey	Albert Culley	
Harold Killick	Eric Porter	

"They shall grow not old as we that are left grow old. Age shall not weary them nor the years condemn.
At the going down of the sun and in the morning We will remember them."

The Right Rev. Charles Gore DD, Bishop of Oxford on March 30th 1919 dedicated the Memorial Cross at 5.40 p.m.

Inglewood Cottage

by Joyce Warne (née Moss)

I was nine when I came to Kintbury in 1941. We – that is Mum and Dad, three sisters (two older, one younger) and on older brother, were evacuees from Portsmouth. We lived at Inglewood Cottage, which was a lovely old house on the edge of the village at the bottom of a hill where three roads meet. Inglewood Cottage, the very name spells enchantment, was a wonderful place to live for we had a huge garden for play, and an apple tree to climb. Distant cornfields glistened under a hot summer sun in skies, which seemed endlessly blue. My sisters and I swam in the local canal, then free of narrow boats and polluted water, took to playing cricket and rounders in the High Street with no fear of traffic and played hide-and-seek amongst the corn stooks. Best of all, in spring were the picnics in the bluebell woods, eating strawberry jam sandwiches and drinking lemonade made with a bright yellow powder which fizzed when water was added. Oh! The days of yesteryear. Where have they all gone?

Kintbury was bliss after the bombs of Pompey, where we spent most nights crouching in our Anderson Shelter and some days also, as there were fearful air raids with much devastation.

Soon after our arrival at Inglewood Cottage, the vicar of St. Mary's called to see us. Then what a surprise! For it was the very same Rev. Guthrie Allison who had christened my sister Betty years before at St. Mary's Church, Portsmouth. What a coincidence, same person, same name of church!

The solitary cottage was deliciously cool in the summer time but an icebox in the winter. Sometimes it was days before the frosted patterns on the sash-type windows went away, after which howling, bitter cold winds found their way down the chimney, through the keyholes and every opening there was and of which there were plenty. On raw wet days we used to huddle round the black range getting toasted on one side only while our backs shivered.

Our water came from an indoor well in the flagstoned scullery. A bucket of water went nowhere for our family of seven so one heard the constant clanging of the chain which hauled the swaying bucket to the surface, splashing everything in its path, including mother's sensible shoes and thick stockings. A huge thick wooden protective cover then dropped back over the deep well with a thud that echoed all over the house. To this day I can still hear that dull, heavy sound. In the corner of the pokey kitchen was a huge stone copper with a fireplace underneath. On wash days the steam would rise in great clouds while mother pummelled away at the cotton sheets and pillowcases, towels, etc. with an enormous copper stick and a bar of Sunlight soap. Soap powders of the day were Rinso, Persil and Oxydol.

Milk and Watercress

Near to Inglewood Cottage were the watercress beds where for sixpence ($2^1/2$p), you could buy a giant bunch of fresh cress to take home for tea. The salad cress was bunched together with a piece of orangey string finished with a loop for carrying. Eaten with crusty Hovis from Mr. Bowsher's bread shop, never did watercress taste so good. Up the hill from the cottage was Sycamore Farm, where again for sixpence, we could get a large jug of creamy milk straight from the cow. When it was my turn to fetch the milk I could never resist taking a small sip from the enamel jug while walking back down the hill to home.

School

Us younger ones went to St. Mary's School (the old building), while the two older ones went to work in the 'Feathery Flake' flour mill down by Kintbury Station. In those far-off days great trucks delivered the fine flour to shops and businesses all over Southern England. I was nervous of school because of my stammer, which was truly dreadful. Perhaps the bombing raids of Portsmouth caused it, or could it have been the mastoid operation at the age of seven, which left me with a semi-deaf ear? Or had it something to do with my being born with six fingers on my right hand? Whatever the cause of my terrible stutter, I was determined to conquer it and conquer it I did, even though it took years. At school I found only kindness and understanding and settled in well, making many friends, with whom I am still in contact.

Our teachers were kind but very strict and were sticklers for the three Rs. One teacher in particular had the biggest false teeth I had ever seen which clicked like castanets every time she spoke, but I would add here I mean no disrespect to that learned lady. On the contrary, she was an excellent treacher who was loved by all. Another teacher was rather portly so as to put it and was rather fond of sitting upon the corner of one's desk, that is until she forgot the ink wells had just that morning been replenished. After that, her ample figure sat at her own desk and in her own chair and was wary forever of those tiny pots of ink which caused much hilarity in the classroom. There were no school dinners in those days so we were fortunate enough to live within walking distance of going home to a hot meal every day. Rabbit was often on the menu with lots of fresh vegetables from the garden, followed by a yummy pudding, such as treacle, jam or sultana with custard. All washed down with clear, cold well water. This would sustain any hungry being such as me. In those halcyon school days everyone had free school milk and this was delivered daily in third-pint bottles. When the ground was covered in frost and ice corks topped the tiny bottles, they were to be found thawing out around the coke-burning black tortoise stove in the classroom.

School started with a hymn and finished with prayers. Empire Day on May 24th was honoured yearly. The whole school paraded around the Union Jack which was hoisted in the playground. Cookery classes were held at Hungerford. We had to walk over the bridges to catch a bus at Kintbury crossroads on the A4. I did not enjoy cooking very much but once I did excel at bread-making and my perfect loaf was on display for all to see. I loved the nature walks to Winterly Woods or the Avenue where there was a place to paddle or sit called 'Granny's Door Step'. Does anyone remember this nostalgic place where friends and I spent many happy hours during golden school summer holidays?

The Shop

I left school at 14 and worked for Mrs. J. Abraham in the grocery and provision trade. Our shop was at the end of Church Street next to The Croft. I believe the building is now called Church House and is the home of a famous writer and his equally famous dog. Back in 1946 there were five such food shops, two butchers, a newsagent, an outfitter's, a barber's (where for sixpence I had my hair mop-shaped), several sweet shops, an ironmonger's and coal yard and Mrs. Willoughby's vegetable and fish shop where on Fridays one could get the tastiest fish and chips.

In Mrs. Abraham's shop the work was interesting but quite hard as nearly everything had to be weighed, including sugar, biscuits, rice, dried fruits, oatmeal and soda and other goods too numerous to mention. Butter, lard and sometimes margarine, came in blocks of 28 lbs. Because there was no fridge or freezer, perishable goods such as fats, cheeses and bacon had to be carried down to the cellar at close of business, then lugged up the steps in the morning. Phew! Who would do this work now? There were two shop assistants (I was one) and Mrs. Abraham made three. Now and then a part-timer would come in to help out. We had to skin whole cheeses and slice the bacon on a razor-sharp bacon slicer. I remember the part-timer cutting her finger on this slicing machine, causing one customer to faint in a dead heap upon our tiled floor at the sight of blood. Only the boss (Mrs. Abraham) was allowed to clean the 'rasher machine' as I called it, for its scythe-like slicer was lethal. The lovely old shop as I recall smelt of polish, candles, carbolic soap, mint humbugs, cheese and above this, the Devon Violets scent worn by my boss.

What wonderful-tasting biscuits we served up in those days. Here are a few of the favourites we sold – Huntley & Palmers Cornish Wafers, Ginger Nuts, Breakfast Rusks and Milk & Honey, Carr's Table Water, Jacobs Custard Creams, which melted in your mouth, Peek Frean's Shortcake and a very special digestive called Granola made by McFarlane Lang. The shop had a doorbell over the top of the door which sounded every time a customer entered. Our motto was 'Service with a Smile' and everyone was greeted with a 'Good Morning' or 'Good Afternoon', whichever applied. Thursday was half-day closing.

Rationing

Rationing was on and the allowance for each person per week was:

8 oz. sugar	2 oz. lard
4 oz. margarine	3 oz. cheese
2 oz. butter	4 oz. bacon

plus one egg and 4 oz. of tea. One dear lady said, "I eat my meagre piece of cheese all in one go as it is better to have one good feed than slice it so thin you can't taste it". Another poor soul walked all of two miles back to the shop on a boiling hot day to return her egg, which was bad, in a cup. Dressed in black to her ankles and wearing

Joyce Moss, Mrs. Abraham and Rachel Culley outside the Church Street shop, decorated for Queen Elizabeth II's Coronation 1953.

a wide-brimmed straw hat this lovely elderly lady said with such sweetness, "I was so looking forward to my weekly egg for tea". She was not disappointed. After a rest in one of the chairs down by the counter, plus a glass of water to refresh her, she went home with two new-laid eggs from Mrs. Abraham's own hens.

Because of food shortages, mother's sister in Australia sent us goody parcels containing lard, honey, jam, bacon, fruit and luncheon meats. These items were most welcome. They helped to stretch our measly rations. Looking back now I often wonder how we all managed on such sparse rations. But we did and people were cheerful as well as good-natured and humble. At least those were who came in our shop. I swept and dusted, filled shelves, weighed up, delivered baskets of shopping on foot, fetched and carried from the cellar. All for the princely sum of 12 shillings (60p) per week. My weekly wage. Oh! I almost forgot to mention the sweet ration, which was 4 oz. per week. This was torture for most children, including me, so when my friends and I had used our sweet coupons up we bought Rennies indigestion tablets to eat, as they were the nearest things to mints. Can you imagine it? These we chewed while idling away time along by the river in glorious weather.

The Coronation Hall and the British Legion Hut

There was no television in our early lives so most evenings were spent listening to the radio. Favourite programmes were ITMA ('It's that man again!'), Dick Barton Special Agent and the Paul Temple series. Once a month there was a dance at the British Legion hut, which was near the Coronation Hall. These dances were highly popular with people coming in from miles away to enjoy a very fine evening of dancing. I remember two outstanding bands which performed there, one was called 'The Barn Owls' and the other 'The Gold Stars'. Dances of the day were the valeta, quickstep, foxtrot, samba, rumba, and if one was skilled enough the tango, to name but a few. The Coronation Hall also held its fair share of dances, including Old Tyme dancing, which was well attended, not only by the dancers themselves but also by people who sat and watched and listened to the music. Concerts were also held with lots of local talent taking part, including my younger sister, Mavis, who had a lovely singing voice.

The VJ party, celebrating the end of the second world war, was held in the Coronation Hall. Bunting was strung across the hall and underneath sandwiches, cakes and jellies were laid out on long trestle tables. Mother helped make the large bowls of jelly. I can see them now as she put them to set on a marble slab in the larder.

We also had a 'Girl's Club' back in the early fifties. This was held in the Parish Room on a Monday evening. From an old piano in the corner of the room one girl rattled out musical tunes for a sing-along and one of our favourite songs was 'Deep In The Heart Of Texas'. We gathered in the Parish Room for talks and discussions on whatever was topical. There were about 20 or so of us to plan the coming events, such as dances, plays, fencing matches, quizzes and card games. We had a marvellous compère for our dances by the name of Mr. B. Harrison of Hungerford.

Autumn

Autumn was my favourite time when I lived at Kintbury. Perhaps it was something to do with the magnificent copper beeches surrounding Inglewood Cottage, for it was then that the trees took on the most glorious hues of red, amber and orange. The colours were a joy to behold. Followed by yet more joy as the tall beeches discarded their tired leaves for me to shuffle through. Another reason why I loved the autumn was Harvest Festival in the little chapel. I can visualise now the pyramid of fruit and variety of vegetables on display. Smell the earthy goodness of the sheaves of corn in the packed chapel as we stood to sing 'We plough the fields and scatter'. Our contribution to this fine produce was from our Blenheim apple tree, which yearly yielded a massive crop of scrumptious eating apples. Inside Inglewood Cottage bowls of eating apples were everywhere, the lovely smell of these delicious apples permeated the house. Outside in a cardboard box were windfalls for people to help themselves.

The evening following Harvest Festival, all of the delicious goods, i.e. jams, jellies, pickles, beans, tomatoes, beetroots, onions, potatoes and breads were auctioned off in the chapel. Buttoned up against the chill night air my sister and I, along with mother, would go to this sale of produce where for just a few pence one could fill a very large bag full of fruit and vegetables. To this day my sisters and I still talk about Mrs. Willoughby's Harvest Festival.

A Step from Kintbury

I lived in the village until the fifties, when I got married in St. Mary's Church and moved to Newbury. However, I am still in contact with the village because my family settled there and I am only a step from Kintbury myself.

Kintbury in Good Voice

by Heather Turner

Until 1954, it had been the practice to appoint to St. Mary's School a Head Teacher who was able as well to act as organist and choirmaster to St. Mary's Church, the last person to hold this dual role being John Bull. This was an advantage in that potential choirboys could be 'selected' from the pupils at the school. So, for the first half of the century, Kintbury was never short of a good supply of talent for the choir and later many went on to join the men's section. The ladies played their part too and though we know little of what happened in earlier days, Kintbury had both choirs and choral society, often the same people, from the late thirties onwards. However it was not until about 1950 that the Choral Society under its then conductor, Renée Stewart, entered its most creative period. At that time the group numbered about 20 men and women. They regularly took part with other local choirs in the Newbury Music Festival and won several awards. They have continued ever since, although numbers have reduced to about 15 and there is rather a shortage of male singers. Their present conductor is Jeremy Plummer, our Vicar's husband and they still participate annually in the festival and the music they tackle very successfully is as ambitious as ever.

Other village groups have burst into song at times over the years, usually in order to raise money for good causes. Pantomimes have always provided a fine opportunity and there have been some good voices heard here over the years. Going back a little, the Girls' Club regularly went carol singing and put on stage shows, and so did a group of slightly older ladies who held concerts and went carol singing to raise money for the 'Old Folks Teas' which they also organised. Also, dare I mention 'The Spreaders', a raucous group of male singers given to singing 'earthy songs' with straw in their hats and dressed in smocks and gaiters. They are still with us today, although mostly retired from the singing scene, but occasionally, with a great deal of persuasion, they give us another public performance, which is always highly acclaimed!

Boys and girls still keep up the tradition of carol singing, with varying degrees of success, as often their repertoire is a touch limited, stretching to no more than the first verse of a couple of carols at most. Going back a few years there was one gang of enterprising young boys who, not having a decent singer between them, hit on the wheeze of going out with a 'wind-up gramophone' and one rather worn record of *Hark the Herald Angels Sing*, or something similar. Unfortunately it does not appear to have been entirely successful and was soon abandoned. One thing is sure, we shall, those of us who are able, go on singing into the next century!

St. Mary's Choir at a local wedding in 1953.

Kintbury at Play

by Heather Turner

From the beginning of the century right up to the present day Kintbury people have been involved in organised sport. The earliest event of which we have a photograph was a Tug of War that was staged round about 1900 in which local railway workers took part and won. We don't know who the other competitors were but judging by the facial expressions of those in the picture they were well satisfied with the result. Another very early photo (1907) is of the Kintbury Quoits Team and they too had just won a competition. At that time this game was played on a court at the back of the Barley Mow Pub (now the home of James and Liz Barnett).

'Newbury Weekly News' reports before and just after the First World War refer at some length to the fact that Kintbury had a reputation for being good at organising and competing in athletics – only it was called 'sports' then. No outdoor event in the village was complete without its 'sports' event for adults and for children.

The other organised games played on a competitive basis from before 1900 were cricket and football. We had no Recreation Ground then and so these were played either at Barton Court or at Wallingtons and this was so right up to the 20s. It was likely though that football was often played much nearer to the village, probably in the Holt Road area which was then just open fields. After the First World War it became obvious due to the popularity of these sports that better facilities were needed and so began the laying out of our present Recreation Ground with funds and land provided by Mr. Arthur Steuart Gladstone, who probably has been our greatest local benefactor of this century. At first facilities for playing cricket and football were provided, together with an open-fronted pavilion which in later years became a splendid 'shelter' on the children's play area. Sadly, due to excessive vandalism, it had to be demolished a few years ago but is missed because it provided excellent shelter when rain threatened.

Mr. Gladstone then went on to complete his plans to provide Kintbury with its beautifully laid out Recreation Ground. When completed it had a large joint Cricket and Football Pitch – which was also to be available for public events like Fetes and Flower Shows and also for organised Children's Games. Additionally, a Bowling Green and three grass Tennis Courts were provided plus a Quoits Court. Bowls, Cricket/Football and Tennis all had their own sturdy brick-built pavilions all finished to a high standard. The whole site was then landscaped with the

planting of trees and beech and laurel hedges. There was no other village in West Berkshire with such a comprehensive and immaculately kept recreation area. All this work was done in the early 1920s and in August 1926 Mr. Gladstone announced to the Parish Council that all the work had been completed and the new Recreation Ground could be handed over to the village.

A Trust Deed with details of how the Recreation Ground was to be managed had been drawn up in the previous year and was so clear and precise that it still holds good today. The only change which has been made is that whereas the original Trustees were well-known local people, (Mr. Gladstone himself, General Rennie, Col. Walmsley and Mr. Goodhart), today's Trustees are the current members of the Parish Council. A small sum of money was invested by Mr. Gladstone which, in 1926 and for some years to come, was sufficient to provide an income which paid the wages of a full-time groundsman, which is why, up to the time of the Second World War, the grounds were kept in such good condition. The clubs were responsible for running and looking after their own playing areas, with the help of the groundsman, and they had to make an annual contribution towards general upkeep. The groundsman at that time and until after the war was Harry Farmer whom many will remember. He was a very knowledgeable man, also Verger of St. Mary's Church and formerly Electrician at Barton Court.

After the war unfortunately the grounds became rather run down. A full-time groundsman could no longer be afforded, membership of the Bowls and Tennis Clubs declined and trouble arose between the Cricket and Football Clubs relating to their joint use of one pitch. The difficulty here was that due to the increasing popularity of football, the season had to be extended to complete match fixtures and so overlapped the cricket season. Annually the Management Committee had to get the two clubs together and declare dates on which handovers must take place.

In reality, it was no longer practical for the two clubs to share the same ground. It is said that around that time some moves were made to extend the ground so that each club could have its own pitch, but unfortunately nothing came of this and the matter was resolved when the Cricket Club ceased to function which was rather sad. Some efforts were made to revive the club in recent years, using a pitch at the Health Hydro, but this did not last through insufficient interest. Cricketers living in Kintbury now go out to other clubs to play.

Meanwhile we nearly lost our Bowling Green, most of which was allowed to become derelict and at the same time the Tennis courts deteriorated and became almost unplayable. However, in recent years, encouraged by the

Kintbury railway workers Tug of War team c1900.

Kintbury Cricket team c1910 after cup win on home ground – 'Flower Show' Meadow.

Parish Council in its role as Trustees and aided by various grants, plus the enormous efforts of members, the Bowling Green is back in order. Hard surfaces have been laid for the Tennis Courts and pavilions have been improved, modernised and extended. This is particularly so with the Football Pavilion which has now separate changing facilities for home and away teams as well as for the referees. It also has a social area and a licensed bar, as does the Bowls Pavilion.

Although football has been played here throughout the century, it was not until 1943 that Kintbury Rangers were formed. For several years they have played in the Hellenic League and their ground was improved with floodlighting and other amenities to accommodate this. From the 1999 season they have rejoined the North Berks League, in which they played before joining the Hellenic. Both Bowls and Tennis Clubs also play in leagues or competitions with other clubs.

Encouraged by an original small grant from the local Queen Elizabeth II Jubilee Fund, the decision was taken to build a small Indoor Sports Hall and so the Jubilee Centre was built on the Recreation Ground, aided by many grants. Controversial at the time of building and still so to some extent, it has provided facilities for many different sports and activities needing more space than could be provided at the Coronation Hall. Competition from nearby recently built larger and better equipped halls is currently causing some concern to the Kintbury Centre.

Reverting to Grounds Maintenance, part-time Groundsman, George Smith has retired this year (1999) after 20 years in the job and will be greatly missed. George regularly put in many more hours than those for which he was paid just because he took such pride in his work. He also had a wonderful way with the children who used the 'Rec', some of whom could be difficult to handle at times. George would reason with them and mostly ended up earning their respect and with them doing what he wanted.

Before the Second World War, tennis was a very fashionable game with the Middle Classes and so it was common for most large houses to have tennis courts. The playing of tennis was then much more a social activity rather than a serious sport. It was a good way for young women to meet up with the opposite sex in the rather more restricted society of those days. The tennis court at 'Fairview' (now Roy and Carol Green's home) was a favourite gathering place for some, the Dopsons whose house it was, having three daughters!

Inevitably Kintbury, with its plentiful rivers, streams and the canal, has always had fishing as a popular leisure activity. Currently there is an Angling Club whose members fish a stretch of the canal and virtually all the other waters are privately fished. In earlier days tackle was very basic, especially for children, and was often home-made and not far away from the proverbial bent pin and a piece of string for, in many cases, this was all that could be afforded. It is very different now, when quite small boys can be seen making for the canal lugging an assortment of lines, nets, containers and many other gadgets which appear to be necessary to catch fish today.

Swimming, bathing and paddling were very popular here in the river and canal, until recent years and the advent of several well-equipped pools within easy distance. Many learned to swim in the 'Sheep Dip' near Shepherd's Bridge at Irish Hill. They were taught by parents, other adults and, more often than not, by older children. Other favourite spots were under the Vicarage Bridge, at Green Lane (Orchard Bridge) and also 'Tumbling Bay'. This is in Hamstead Marshall Parish near Dreweatts Lock, where sluices control water leaving the canal. One had to be a strong swimmer and careful here because it could be dangerous. Those children too young or not able to swim 'paddled' in shallower waters and 'going paddling' usually involved a picnic tea and was great fun on hot summer days. In winter, if we had enough snow there was a flurry of activity at 'The Firs' on Blandys Hill when many hastily made toboggans appeared from nowhere and there were many thrills and spills. Netball was played by girls at St. Mary's School between the wars and organised sports have always been a feature of our schools' activities. Netball has also fairly consistently been played by women's teams in Kintbury.

Turning to indoor activities, dancing as you might expect has always been a popular pastime. The 'Sixpenny Hops' of the 20s and 30s have been mentioned elsewhere and David Morris, who lived in Kintbury then remembers that french chalk was put down on the floor of the Hall in the afternoon and two boys sat on a sack which was then pulled across the room to get a good shine on the floor ready for dancing in the evening. In the 30s there was another innovation. Instead of having a band to play for the dancing, which could become expensive and sometimes not easy to obtain, we had 'Mr. Razey and his Radiogram' – surely the forerunner of today's 'D.J.'!

There were other forms of dancing too. Maypole dancing was taught in the local schools but seemed to die out during or after the Second World War. After the war classes were started in 'Country Dancing' and this became popular not only here but in other local villages, and summer parties were held when dancers from these groups got together to 'Strip the Willow' and perform other dances with equally odd names. A favourite gathering

Kintbury Football Club, local league winners 1933, outside first pavilion, now demolished.

place was the lawn at Wheatlands Farm, Enborne, where the music provided by piano and violin would waft out of the sitting room window and the dancers would cavort till dusk and then go home exhausted by this burst of unusual activity! The Kintbury team, of whom I was one, had a 'uniform'. This was made out of blackout curtain material – a gathered skirt with stripes of coloured bias binding sewn on, for this was just after the war and clothes rationing was still in force.

A little later, Miss Whalley, then Headmistress of Christchurch School, started 'Old Time Dancing' in the classroom there. This later transferred to the Coronation Hall with proper instruction and this, too, became popular with some older members of the community who remembered similar dances from their youth.

Much nearer to our own time, Penny Brookman became interested in Morris Dancing and it is her we have to thank for the formation of the Kintbury May Maids – still going strong today – and for introducing the village to a modern celebration of the early May Bank Holiday. Penny tells her own story in the two short articles which follow this one.

To bring dancing right up to date, we do of course have discos, line dancing and even the odd 'Ball' but to complete nostalgia for past pleasures we have the return of the 'Tea Dance', organised by a dedicated group of 'Volunteers' and patronised by an equally dedicated group of very competent dancers.

Mention must be made of less physically active ways leisure time was spent in Kintbury. Though few in earlier days there are now many clubs and most of these have separate chapters in this book so no need to comment here. Whist Drives are worth a mention. These were enormously popular throughout the first part of the century and would frequently completely fill the Coronation Hall. A former storeroom used to be stacked with folding green baize-covered tables for this purpose. Likewise the Parish Room had its stack of tables. Those who had had a good night at the tables would come home satisfied and clutching prizes. A bad night meant you had been dealt a 'rotten hand', had a 'useless partner' – or both. It never had to do with your own poor play! Highlight each year was the huge 'Fur and Feather' Drive, when prizes were scrounged from all the local landowners and many a Christmas Dinner was won. Whist is still played today on a much more modest scale, usually once a fortnight, alternating with Bingo. However another card game, Bridge, is increasing in popularity and weekly sessions are held at the Coronation Hall.

This leaves us, almost where we began – with pubs and their pastimes, but no longer Quoits at the Barley Mow. Darts, Music and other entertainments – or just 'chat' now make regular visits to the 'Ball', 'Dundas' or 'Prince' popular for many Kintbury people. In 1900 we had eight pubs, now we have only these three – long may they continue into the new century!

Kintbury May Maids Morris

The Kintbury May Maids was formed in 1982 to dance at the village May Day Festival. Penny Brookman had been teaching Maypole dancing to the children and suggested that some of the parents should dance as well. In 1983 the team joined the Morris Federation and performed at the Federation's annual meeting in Stratford upon Avon.

With additional tuition and music from local teacher Helen Howlett, the side developed its repertoire and in 1986 we were invited to dance the traditional 'Dummer Five Hand Reel' at a fete in the Hampshire village of Dummer, opened by the future Duchess of York and her then fiance Prince Andrew. This launched us onto national news, a special TVS programme from Dummer, on the eve of the Royal Wedding, and our international debut with a feature for Japanese Breakfast TV. Consequently the highlight of 1987 was a trip to Osaka, Japan, to represent Great Britain in the international Midosudji parade where over 100 foreign groups, together with thousands of Japanese, provided a colourful spectacle which was relayed live, by television, throughout Japan and the Pacific, with over a million spectators on the streets. We were invited to return to Japan in 1998, but due to the illness and subsequent death of Emperor Hirohito, the trip was postponed until 1989.

In 1990 we were invited by Newbury Twin Town Association to travel to Braunfels in W. Germany, for a Medieval fair in the nearby village of Phillipstein, to celebrate the 600th anniversary of its castle, along with other local groups and teams from associated twin towns throughout Europe.

The last few years have included a diverse selection of events and festivities, including dancing at fetes, weddings, barn-dances, christening a pub and a boat (with new dances added to the repertoire to honour the occasions). We have also danced at an international festival in London on the Queen's official birthday, with time off to wave as the royal party went by, and danced in procession with hundreds of other Morris dancers, to Downing Street, where our May Queen joined the party presenting a petition to save the May Day holiday.

In 1994 we flew to New England as guests of 'Mystic Garland', a team who had visited us in July 1988, and shared our traditions with dancers from New York to Boston, culminating in performances at the Canterbury Fair, New Hampshire.

In 1997, May Maids were proud to represent women's Morris Dance teams in the making of a video, in Oxford, to promote Morris Dancing to schools, and involving representatives of the three governing bodies of Morris tradition in England. The video has since been shown on BBC television and is on sale through BBC publications.

At Easter 1998 we flew to Ispra, Italy, to dance for representatives of the EEC at their research centre, and later that year, whilst performing in the village of Fougerolles Du Plessis in France, were asked to present bouquets to winners of a regional heat of the 'Tour de France'.

As we approach the Millennium, Kintbury May Maids Morris is known and respected both nationally and internationally and continues to draw new members from its village base as well as the surrounding area. Some of the group, including founder member Penny Brookman, have been with the side for years, and past members who have moved away still return to dance from farther afield. The side which was formed to dance for one event in the village calendar is still an integral part of those May Day festivities, and in recent years has started a new tradition of dancing at dawn on 1st May.

Kintbury May Day Festivities

Kintbury's May Day festivities represent a traditional celebration which has long since disappeared from many towns and villages, but which has been recorded for many generations in this area.

Village dancing classes had for some years included maypole and garland dances and seasonal performances for parents at the Coronation Hall, and Mrs Milnes-Walker had been teaching Longsword dancing to boys, but only in 1977 for the Queen's Jubilee celebrations, did the children maypole dance in Church Street at the Street Fair.

Penny Brookman was the dancing teacher at the time, and with a supportive group of parents began to develop the tradition. Over the years several generations of boys and girls have performed maypole, garland, longsword, Cotswold and Border Morris dances to an audience of parents, friends and visitors, and the Kintbury May Maids. Morris was originally a group of mums who learnt a few dances to surprise the children, but have been an integral feature ever since! The format of the day has only changed slightly over the years, and still involves dancing for the elderly residents of

The original Kintbury May Maids in May 1982.

'Notrees', and a performance outside the church where the crowning of the May Queen takes place, although in 1999 the first May King was crowned. Originally the festivities took place on the first Saturday in May, but have occurred on the 'May Day' Bank Holiday Monday since its initiation.

The maypole has been replaced several times, and is currently set-up for the day on the green at Bradley Close, rather than carried around the village as it was in the early days. Current legislation and policing regulations meant that in 1999, for the first time, the children, dancers and musicians were unable to proceed around the village, and had to walk up Inkpen Road to reach the green. The May Queen's transport for many years was a pony and trap but more recently has included a vintage car, a Rolls-Royce and a sports car.

The spirit of the day is still an un-commercialised traditional family and village event. It is the children's day but everyone participates to ensure that music and dance, provided by local people for the entertainment of local people, is a focal point of the Spring calendar. A tradition which is very much a part of Kintbury will hopefully delight for many more generations, as a living, developing tradition.

May Day 2000 actually takes place on Monday 1st May.

A Dog's Life in Kintbury

by Dido Chapman Pincher

Recently, I heard some pop star belly-aching on TV about the price of fame and the problem of being recognised and mobbed by fans and having their privacy invaded. Let me confess that I love being recognised in the street when being walked by my Chap in and around Kintbury. Children rush up to me calling out 'There's the dog that writes books!' Or 'Hello Dido! Written any good books lately?' I love it for I'm no Garbo and never want to be alone except when I am man-tired and need a sleep.

The first evidence that I was really famous was when the Chap and I were visiting a remote place called the Pass of Killicrankie in the Highlands of Scotland. Having visited the site of the famous battle there – between humans, not a dog-fight – the Chap said 'Come on, Dido', to which an elderly lady immediately responded 'That's not *the* Dido is it?' It turned out that she was a fan of my first book, *One Dog and Her Man*, lived in Edinburgh and loved Labradors, especially chocolate ones like me. But that was nothing compared with what happened when that book was published in Japanese and sold 50,000 hard-back copies in Japan, swelling the joint bank account the Chap and I have at Lloyds in Hungerford. The British Embassy in Tokyo were so impressed that they decided to feature me in the glossy annual they publish to promote British exports to Japan and encourage Japanese tourism here. Having telephoned the Chap, who secured my agreement, they sent a Japanese journalist to interview me in Church House, Kintbury and a Japanese photographer from London even took pictures of my torn-up football. When the annual came out the Prime Minister, then John Major, had only one page in it but I had four. I was barking for Britain! Now, I have my entry in the *International Who's Who of Animals*. (Honest! But it would have to be an American publication, wouldn't it?)

It is surprising whom I meet in Kintbury. One morning, an elderly couple who had been staying at St. Mary's House noticed my unusual colour and stopped the Chap to ask about my breed. They turned out to be Americans and were even more surprised to learn of my literary achievement in presenting the dog-man relationship in such a challenging way and when they heard that I had just had seven chocolate pups they asked to see them. Shortly after their return to America,

the man, who turned out to be a poet, wrote a clever sonnet which ended:

'The world may deem me poor, but I am rich
Because I've met you: charming chocolate bitch.'

My poet annotated his lines with paw-notes explaining that it would be in *The Tales of Hoffdog* that he would love to hear me bark a role. To that my immediate response was 'No problem! I Offenbach.' (Game, set and match!)

The couple still write regularly and I get fan mail from other countries, some addressed simply to 'Dido, Kintbury, Berks' which reaches me with no delay. Sometimes treats come through our front door, either by post or when people knock to have their books signed.

Most writers have to visit their publishers, usually in London, but when they become really famous their publishers have to visit them. My publishers – I have had several because of the paperback versions – always visit me, which is just as well because I hate London, though I sometimes have to make a sacrifice and go there for book-signings (which I do with my paw-print) at posh places like Harrods and Hatchards in Piccadilly. I have even been to Birmingham (which is worse) to sign books when I appeared in the Parade of Dog Personalities at the great Cruft's dog show. It was a great honour, I suppose, but when I got back to Kintbury I wrote a little poem of my own:

Oh Kennet banks are fair and wide with lots of reeds and tufts.
I'd rather roam with my Chap there than reign the Queen of Cruft's!

My Chap and I do a lot of roaming together on the Kennet's banks, either walking around Kintbury but, more often, fishing at Littlecote. Most people don't know it but we Labradors were first bred as fishing dogs. The sea-fishermen of nearby Newfoundland wanted dogs

The author
Sculpture of Dido by William Newton of Kintbury

that would retrieve the cod which fell off their long-lines, baited with many hooks, when they dragged them in. We needed to be strong swimmers, tough to withstand the cold sea and able to retrieve the cod without damaging them. So fishing is in my blood and I can retrieve a trout when the Chap has played it out. (He won't let me have a go at a salmon when we are on our Scottish trips though I'd love to try.)

Being a dog of so many parts, I am in local demand to open fairs and fêtes for which we have invented an ingenious device. Usually, they like me to cut a ribbon when I am opening something, such as the extension to a school, as I did in Chilton Foliat, and to make this easier – and more worthwhile for me – we thread the ends of two lengths of stiff ribbon through a slit in a cooked sausage. On the command 'Open!' I seize the sausage and the ribbon falls apart. I have never muffed it, so far, but anyone else attempting this should always have a back-up sausage at the ready. We always do and, of course, I get that too.

Naturally, such events are covered by the media, usually the Newbury Weekly News when the photographer, my friend Peter Bloodworth, adds to my thick album of photographs which contains several of my sausage act in Kintbury and round about. Occasionally, I give my charitable services further afield, once as far away as Slough where I did a double act with the famous Dulux dog. Like him, I have also appeared on TV – even on the Big Breakfast Show to promote my block-buster called *Life's A Bitch!* I have been painted and etched and even sculpted in bronze – by Willie Newton, our famous village sculptor who used to specialise in horses but decided that he would like to model me for one of his London exhibitions. He came into our garden when I was chasing around with a full-size football, which the Boss (as we both call the Chap's wife) had bought me. I over-ran the ball and, for a split second, all four legs were off the ground with the ball supporting my chest and Willie caught the moment in modelling clay and then in bronze. The Boss liked it so much that she bought a copy for the Chap's birthday so that there is no way he can escape me. Poor old fellow! I suppose that my second greatest achievement on behalf of my species has been to cut my Chap down to size by converting him to my ghost-writer, presenter, secretary, interpreter, minder, chauffeur and general dogsbody or, as he calls it, adoguensis. 'Are you the man who owns that famous dog?' is now a common question to which he replies, mournfully, 'No. She owns me.' I see his point because, while it is bad enough for a professional author to be outsold by his wife, to be outsold by his bitch must be really demoralising.

The Author and The Chap in Church Street, 1998

So what is my first greatest achievement? Well that, too, happened in Kintbury, right by the Church, in fact. I had received a letter of thanks and congratulations from the Queen after I had sent her a copy of my first book but I had never met her and was determined to do so. After the Boss had collected a lot of money to buy a church bell dedicated to Sir Gordon Richards, the famous jockey, she induced Her Majesty to visit our church and take part in the dedication ceremony. The Boss and the Chap had to be with her but we arranged things so that I would be standing just outside the gate when they all emerged and the Boss could say 'Oh look, there's Dido!'

It worked a treat. 'So that's Dido, is it?' the Queen said as I was presented and did my version of a canine curtsy. 'You don't see many chocolates.'

Not many dogs have ambushed the Monarch and got away with it!

Young Kintbury

by Heather Turner

How young people in Kintbury spent their time during this century is quite interesting and mirrors the tremendous change there has been in lifestyle. Before and around 1900 there seems to have been no organised groups for children or young people in the village. It was Agnes Edwards, daughter of the Reverend Edwards and usually known as 'Cowboy Aggie' who started the first group and those belonging were known as 'The King's Messengers'. This was for young boys and girls and had a religious basis with an expected code of conduct. George Smith, who lived in Church Street then, was one of Aggie's 'Messengers'. Somehow though, on one occasion he got the message wrong when curiosity took him up into the church belfry. Unfortunately the Reverend Edwards caught him up there which resulted in a severe reprimand and an allocated punishment. This was to sweep the churchyard paths for one week. George says that he got so interested in the task that he carried on sweeping after the week was up!

Agnes Edwards was also the Cubmistress when the first Cub Group was formed. We don't know the date of this, nor when the first Scout troop was formed. However, we think the Scouts started well before the First World War. We have a picture of the Kintbury Scouts Bugle Band dated 1914 and it is obvious from this that they were well established then. In fact we had Scouts here before Newbury. The Cub Movement was founded nationally in 1916 and it must have been very soon after that we had our first Cubs. The booklet published by Newbury & District Scouts for their Diamond Jubilee Year, 1967, throws little light on what happened to Scouts and Cubs here between the two wars but for most of this time the groups continued and also on through the Second World War. However by 1956 there was no Scout Troop, although the Cubs seem to have continued. It was then that Mr. D. Cummins, local policeman, restarted the group and they then became the First Inkpen and Kintbury Scouts. Since then there have been a number of different Scoutmasters, among them and well remembered were Douglas Connah and Bill Jenkins. Leader since 1987 has been Ivan Osborne and his wife, Mary, is Cub Leader. Currently Scout numbers average 15 and Cubs 20. The Scouts have had three different homes since their formation in addition to temporary use of other buildings. Their first was at Osmington Farm in Wallingtons Road where they had a large wooden building, probably ex-World War One. This had a Second World War history too

in that it was used by other groups then for concerts and other things. Also it was used by the Home Guard as a 'First Aid Post' during their mock battles when some Scouts, with handkerchiefs tied round their arms, acted as 'Messengers'. The story is often told locally of the Home Guard who got 'wounded' during the battle so was sent to the First Aid Post. The rest of the force, absorbed in their war game, forgot about him for some time and when they remembered to send someone to attend to his 'injuries' he had disappeared leaving a note on the door 'Bled to death – gone home'. The Scouts' next headquarters was another wooden hut on land now part of Great Severals where they operated for many years after the Second World War. When this land was acquired for development, they moved to their present site off Gainsborough Avenue and a new hut. Currently both Scouts and Cubs follow an energetic programme of activities, including 'camps' under the guidance of their leaders, Ivan and Mary, who devote much of their spare time to the Movement. Activities also include money-raising through mammoth jumble sales and providing barbecued food at the Annual Street Fayre and similar occasions.

One Kintbury family (shown above) has had four generations in the Guide Movement in Kintbury. Elsie Child (née White), the blacksmith's daughter, was a Guide in its very early days. Her daughter, Joan Sadler, was a Brownie and a Guide, whilst her daughter, Sarah Knibbs, was a Brownie and Guide and now runs Kintbury Brownies. Victoria Perkins, her daughter, the fourth generation, was a Brownie and Guide and now the Brownie Assistant Guider.

The first Guide Pack was formed in 1915, followed by Brownies in 1925, and a colourful description of their activities over the years, written by the current Guide Leader, Judy Wilson, follows this chapter.

In the 1920s and 1930s, at what is now the home of Colin and Margaret Bailey at 23 Church Street, there was what was then known as the Working Men's Club. It was also known as the 'Reading Room', having been set up by the Reverend Edwards and was where children were sent from St. Mary's School to borrow books – a forerunner of the Public Lending Library which was to come to the village later. Not a lot is known about the Men's Club activities but it was a place where young men could meet socially. There is no record and no-one can remember any similar club for the girls of the village.

Between the wars, Sunday Schools organised by St. Mary's Church and the Chapels, were well attended. It is probable that almost every child aged five to 12-plus went to one or other of these. Parents of that generation insisted that their children should attend – even if they themselves rarely worshipped. They considered it important that their young should be properly instructed about religion. For the children themselves – there were incentives! These took the form of summer outings and Christmas tea parties. It was not unknown for some children to switch 'faith' in order not to miss a treat! Sunday Schools also ran Savings Clubs into which the children paid a few coppers each week, provided by their parents and this was marked off on a savings card. Once or twice a year these cards were 'made up' with a bonus called 'interest' which in reality was a little extra donated by local benefactors from among the 'better off'. Parents would then take their children and the cards to clothing shops in Newbury, such as 'Beynons', where new outfits were bought and then paraded on the following Sunday.

During the Second World War there sprang up a 'Girls Club'. It had about 15 members and they met in the Parish Room. Leader was Miss Wake, who was the Surgery Dispenser. They busied themselves with a whole range of activities which varied from carol singing at Christmas to camping. What is remembered most though is the tremendous effort which they put into raising money so that a celebration party could be held for 'the boys' when they returned from the war. Having raised the money they were then much involved in organising the party itself and this is still remembered today with just pride. After the war though the club gradually became less active and eventually folded.

Also during the war another young people's club was formed. This started by Mr. and Mrs. Foster, who were devout Methodists, and had made Haworth House their wartime home, being related to the owner, Miss Corsar, who was herself on war service with the Red Cross. The Fosters felt that there was a need for the children of the village 'to have something more to do'. The club, which was called the 'Kintbury Children's Circle', met weekly in the early evening at Haworth House where religious subjects were explored, usually by selecting a text and examining its meaning. Minimal refreshments were provided as an inducement. After a few meetings, some of the older boys, bored with the proceedings, became somewhat disruptive and so were discouraged from attending. Miffed by their exclusion, they soon renamed the group the 'Kintbury Coffee Cadgers' by which title it is mostly remembered today. As is the case with most children's activities, the novelty wore off and after a fairly short existence the Circle closed down.

And so we come to the Boys' Club. There had in fact been some sort of gathering for boys back in the early 1930s. These were at the room in Station Road which was later taken over by the Parochial Church Council and called the Parish Room. The lady who organised this group was Mrs. Baring from Forbury House. It did not have a leader as such but was a 'facility' where boys could come and play ping-pong, have card games, do boxing and other indoor activities. Mrs. Baring came down and brewed up cocoa on the tortoise stove which the boys could have for a ha'penny a mug to wash down doughnuts at another ha'penny which were a 'special purchase' from Mr. Rolfe's the Bakers (probably stock left over at the end of the day!). It is not known for how long this operated but for some years and until after the Second World War there was no club. It was in 1947, due to the efforts of four enthusiastic Kintbury people – Rodney Palmer, Sir Frank Spickernell, Walter Hobbs and George Palmer that a new Boys' Club was formed. Between 30 and 40 boys became members and they met in a 'tin hut' put up on land, now part of Great Severals. This was heated by a tortoise stove and was the centre of many activities which included boxing, table tennis and drama. Outdoor pursuits were football, a Motor Cycle Club and a Rifle Club. In 1984 the land on which the club's building stood was sold for development and so it moved into a new and larger building off Gainsborough Avenue where it remains today. Since then the clubhouse has been updated with better kitchen and toilet facilities. Also it has a hard-surfaced outdoor sports court suitable for tennis, five-a-side football, basketball and netball.

Over the years many local people have been involved in the running of the club, often because their own children were members. These people took a great interest in club activities and some taught the boys new skills. Bob

(Above) The Girls Club in fancy dress. c1945.

(Below) 1st Kintbury Scouts Bugle Band 1914.

Walker, then the landlord of the *Prince of Wales* gave boxing lessons and Frank Stacey taught carpentry. Some of the boys did well too. Stuart Luker won a Duke of Edinburgh Award, Brian Sampson was noted for his cross-country running and the club built a craft which won the Crafty Craft race.

In 1980 girls were admitted for the first time and so the club was renamed the 'Kintbury Youth Club'. These days the club meets twice a week and has two paid part-time leaders, Jenny Elliott and Veronica Maston. Present trustees are Tony Preston, Raymond Tapkin and Gary Kax. Funds are currently being raised by selling a portion of the site for development so that restoration of the club premises can be completed.

All the foregoing were the formal activities of the young, but they had other ways of passing the time too. Boys made 'camps' in secluded places around the village – and sometimes if they were lucky a few girls were allowed to join in. There was a very popular 'Cycle Speedway' which was held on land where Queens Way is now and here the boys could show off their skills in 'biking' though cycles then were not nearly as manoeuvrable as they are today. Being near water, rafts were made and tested out on the canal. Sometimes they floated, sometimes they didn't! There was a useful pond where Great Severals is now and here one lad took to the water in his mother's tin bath! Soapboxes were made too and there was always a demand for old pram wheels for these. When constructed, testing took place on all the downhill roads in the village – fortunately there was not much traffic then!

Bigger boys, usually those between about 14 and 18, but sometimes older, had what always seemed a rather odd activity. They would stand in considerable numbers on the corner of the Square in the early evening. They rarely did anything, except making the odd remark to passing girls and they were certainly not menacing in any way – they just stood!

Between the wars 'playground games' have been recalled by contributors to this book. Mostly it was girls who took part in these. There were various 'ring games' accompanied by the chanting of rhymes and then there was 'Donkey', a wall ball game which entailed throwing a ball at the wall, letting it bounce, jumping over it at the same time so that it could be caught by the next girl in the team. The boys played leapfrog, 'conkers' if they were in season, and marbles but mostly stood about in groups. Outside school they would play cricket or football, according to the season while the girls played 'hop scotch' or skipping games, usually in the middle of the road!

On Sunday afternoons it was 'family walks' as this was the day when you had to behave yourself and 'do something quiet'. Boys always wore caps then. So, when you met another group out walking, you always had to have respect for the other 'grown ups' so boys got a sharp prod in the back from mother with a hissed whisper, "Raise your cap to Mrs. ....!". It is said, going back somewhat further in the century and to the time when the Edwards family occupied the Vicarage, girls were expected to courtsey to Mrs. Edwards and any other local lady from the 'upper classes'!

Then there was Mrs. Bowen's Tea Party. This lady called regularly at St. Mary's School in the 1930s to distribute the 'Band of Hope' magazine. As a treat, once a year, she invited the school down to Titcombe Manor for tea – which consisted of a cup of tea or a lemonade drink and a ha'penny bun, not very exciting by today's standards, especially as the buns were not always of the freshest. But it was a 'treat' so we mostly went.

At this time, before the Second World War, the biggest excitement for children was the annual visit to the Fair in Hungerford or Newbury. This took place in October, as it still does today. All schoolchildren were given a half day off to go, mainly because they would have gone anyway! Fairs were big then and full of hissing steam engines to drive the roundabouts and other rides.

Just after the Second World War and before television arrived, the highlight of the week for many children, especially the boys, was the Friday night travelling film show at the Coronation Hall. This was always well attended, despite the age of the films shown and the constant breaking down of the projection equipment.

Then came the television age, followed later by home computers, and life for children in Kintbury changed. Many other facilities became available – close-by sports complexes, offering a whole range of activities including fitness training and swimming – so many things from which to choose, so the pastimes of yesteryear have more or less passed away. However, within this village itself, facilities are still somewhat limited. Our Scouts, Guides, Cubs, Brownies and Rainbows flourish and so cater for the younger children but activities for 12 to 18-year-olds seem to be limited to the twice-weekly sessions at the Youth Club. As we leave the 20th Century, perhaps this is an area which we should address with some urgency.

Guiding
by Judy Wilson

"We're off to camp and don't forget your palliasse", that was what one ex-Guide remembers from her days as a pre-war Guide. One cannot imagine the Guides of today being thrilled with that prospect as a palliasse was a hessian sack filled with straw that one had to sleep on!

Kintbury Guides join other local Guides. c1947.

Official records do not extend back to the early days of Guiding in Kintbury, but it is believed that Miss Sawbridge from Denford House started the Guides in 1915, and Mrs. Fraser of Templeton House was running the Guides in 1925. The Brownies were first formally registered in 1925, and run from 1929 until 1978 by Miss Sybil Dobson of Titcomb. Brownies and Guides used to meet in a hay loft at the Vicarage, above a room that housed a bier for the coffins to rest on, moving to Fairview House, Inkpen Road and then the Coronation Hall, with meetings on a Saturday afternoon. The Brownies wore brown dresses whose pockets contained paper and pencil, string, pennies for a telephone call and a clean handkerchief, yellow ties and a woolly hat in winter and a straw hat in summer. Their meetings started by repeating "Twit twoo" three times and on the third time loudly and jumping up in the air. They played games and sat on logs for stories and pow-wows. In summer they played games on 'Brownie Island', on the Kennet and Avon canal, by Vicarage Bridge, and reached it by walking across on a wooden plank.

The Guides wore navy dresses, orange ties, leather belts, lanyards with whistles attached and felt pudding-basin hats, gaining points for their patrol for smartness. The uniforms were often obtained for 1p or 2p, as they were second-, third- or fourth-hand. Their Guider leaders looked very smart in their suits, leather gloves and hats with a cockade on them. Early recollections of Guides include collecting moss to be used as dressings for bandages for the World War I convalescent home at Barton Court. The Guides in the 1930s recall gaining

badges for sewing and cooking, being tested by the Reverend Guthrie Alison's cook, Florrie Ricketts. It is recalled that the test was a meal cooked and served to the Vicar and his cook – of pea soup, lamb chops and vegetables. Guides taking their writer's badge would sit at separate tables at Haworth House just like an exam. In 1937 Kintbury Guides travelled by a special train to Windsor to join all Berkshire Guides in Windsor Great Park to celebrate King George VI's coronation. The King and Queen rode in an open carriage, with the Princesses Elizabeth and Margaret looking very pretty in their straw bonnets. They also attended County Rallies at Newbury Racecourse. The Guides held day camps by Kiln Farm and Inkpen and Combe and occasionally went away to camp. Miss Doris Prince was the Guide Captain for many years and Miss Joyce Greenough her Lieutenant. The Guides had their own Guide Hut, in Wallingtons Road, which was bought with money raised by the Guides. It later ended up in Dr. Gillman's garden as a summer house. Later Guide meetings were held in the Parish Room and now are held in the Coronation Hall. The Guide Company closed several times in the 1960s and 1970s, restarting in 1978, whereas the Brownie Pack has been running continuously since 1925, with Rainbows starting in 1995. Today's Brownies and Guides take part in a full range of activites from first aid to canoeing, climbing and still enjoy traditional hike cooking. The Brownies go away on Pack Holidays and the Guides regularly go camping and have recently attended an International Camp. The Rainbow, Brownie and Guide units continue to thrive in Kintbury.

Ancient Kintbury

Extracts from material supplied by Thora Morrish and Margaret Yates

Our book concerns itself only with the 20th century, past centuries having been well recorded by Thora Morrish and Margaret Yates in their book *1,000 Years of Kintbury* and in their additional lecture notes. However we should mention the 'discoveries' which have been made during this past 100 years.

From the early 1900s up to more recent times, excavations in the lower part of Church Street and Millbank areas have from time to time unearthed skeletons. These have been examined by experts who have confirmed them as the remains of Saxons, which is not surprising as they have all been found in the extensive area east of St. Mary's Church, which is known to be a Saxon burial ground.

In 1960, excavations at Wawcott Farm revealed a Mesolithic (Stone Age) site, dated around 3,300 B.C. with signs of a human settlement and activity in working with flints.

Nearer to the centre of the village, it is not unusual to find what appear to be 'worked' flints on the allotment land at Pound Close.

However, the find of the century was during the years 1948 to 1951, when work connected with the provision of a sewage works for Kintbury to the east of the village and on the south bank of the canal, revealed signs of Roman occupation. Within the sewage plant site itself, pottery, a brooch and coins covering the whole of the Roman occupation of Britain were found. Further excavations by a team led by Douglas Connah, then a teacher at St. Bartholomew's School, in the field next to the sewage works, revealed a 4th century Romano-British building which turned out to be a Roman bath house. Teams explored this site over a three-year period and recorded, as far as they could, the layout of the building. Traces of a mosaic floor were found, and evidence of a heating system, but it was not possible from what remained to identify a clear ground plan. After the three-year project, the site was covered up again. No evidence has been found up to now as to why the building was there but coupled with the finds on the sewage plant site itself, there are strong indications that somewhere in the area was either a Roman villa or a village settlement. Who knows, perhaps sometime in the 21st century, further discoveries will be made and the mystery solved.

Written by Heather Turner, with further material supplied from N.W.N. issue 22nd November 1951. Photography by J. H. Hole, A.R.P.S.

How People Lived

by Heather Turner

Before the First World War Kintbury was very much a self-contained community. Nearly everyone worked within the village, children received all their education at the local schools and people found little need to travel far. There were at least twenty shops, a surgery, eight pubs, four blacksmiths, a wheelwright, two undertakers, three churches and two chapels. In addition there were many local craftsmen, so most needs could be met within Kintbury.

Life was basic for most. Diets consisted of simple foods, meat, cheese, milk, bread and vegetables in season, mostly home grown. Many families kept chickens for their eggs and when they no longer laid, they were eaten. Rabbits were plentiful and some kept a pig or two. Nellie Watts, who lived in part of what is now September Cottage in Church Street kept one in her tiny backyard. This was an adventurous animal who found he could lift the latch on the gate with his snout and was often recaptured down by the church – and on one Sunday evening got into the church and joined 'Evensong'! Nellie was also a great wine maker, as were most families then. Home-made winemaking was far from sophisticated. A curious collection of pans, bowls and jars were used in the process and wine was made of many vegetables grown in the garden, fruits and wild flowers. Favourites were Cowslip, Dandelion, Parsnip and Elderberry. Foreign wines were unheard of for most and the quality of the home brew was judged by 'how much kick it had in it'. It was freely offered when visitors called. Some of it was very potent – but this didn't matter as there were no cars to drive.

It was at about this time that in winter particularly you could get a Soup Dinner at the laundry in High Street for two old pennies – and it was good stuff by all accounts. Faggots and Mushy Peas could be had from the shop behind the Barley Mow, also reckoned to be jolly good!

People were extremely poor in the early 1900s and this was not helped by the recessions of the 20s and 30s. However, because nearly everyone else was too, it was accepted as the way of life and on the whole, people managed. As the century progressed towards the beginning of the Second World War, people were a little better off and there was beginning to be a wider choice of foodstuffs. Some of our shops had gone by then, and one of our pubs – the 'Nags Head' now the home of Nigel and Judy Wilson at the top of Laylands Green. Then came the war and a whole new way of life,

well reported elsewhere so we need not dwell on it here.

Reverting to inter-war years and before, there was no mains water in Kintbury until about 1936 so most houses had their own wells, long since filled in – or most of them are! Some houses had to share and this was particularly so with the pre-war council houses, where in some cases as many as ten shared the same well. But these householders were still better off than those living around Blandys Hill where water had to be fetched by the bucket from a spring near to the former Axe and Compass pub. One man could be seen regularly carrying water for his family using a shoulder yoke to take the weight of his two buckets. When mains water came the situation changed very slowly and as late as the middle 40s some houses still had only well water. In its favour though many people who experienced these early days, praised the quality of the water which they said "made a good cup of tea". When the council houses were first connected to the mains supply, taps were still outside and sometimes shared between two houses. Main drainage did not come to Kintbury until 1948. Though some houses had their own septic tanks, most of the smaller houses, council and privately owned just had 'bucket lavatories'. Sometimes these were part of the main house but always with their own outside door, sometimes they were in an outbuilding opposite the back door and quite often with older houses they were in a purpose made building at the bottom of the garden and quite attractive these latter looked sometimes – viewed from the outside! Whichever type, it was necessary for house occupants to go outside, whatever the weather, to go to the 'loo'. The emptying of the buckets was sometimes done by the householder and sometimes 'contracted out' to someone else which might entail the use of a cart or truck. These acquired odd names disguising their purpose, one mentioned recently being the 'honey cart'! Where the contents removed from the buckets went is also a bit obscure since it was an operation usually carried out at dusk, but often they were buried in gardens or on allotments.

Except for some houses and shops in the centre of the village supplied from about the middle 20s by Mr. Phillips from his Electric Lighting Works, electricity did not come to most homes until the middle 30s and there were some who had to wait another ten years or more before they had a supply. Before that, people used oil lamps, some of them quite elaborate affairs, and these were supplemented by candles. We are, of course, still dependent on candles today when we have our not infrequent power cuts and these give us an insight into just how difficult it must have been to live without electricity. Cooking was done on little kitchen ranges using solid fuel, or a few people used stoves with ovens fuelled by paraffin – but these were extremely smelly affairs. Kintbury did not have gas though it has been strongly rumoured that just about the turn of the century, Col. Walmesley, who was then living at Inglewood Lodge, had the idea of providing himself and the village with a supply of gas which would be manufactured from an outbuilding at Inglewood Lodge and that foundations were dug for a gasometer to store the gas. It is said that the people of Kintbury were not interested in the idea and so it was abandoned. This may be true, bearing in mind the lack of enthusiasm shown for electric street lighting and mains water reported in the Parish Council article in this book. There was certainly a strange, dark building at the Lodge which I think may later have been used to generate electricity, and a large round sunken pond which may have been the gasometer foundations. We shall never know.

Returning to electricity, when this was first installed, it was for lighting only and there were no power points. So, when electrical goods began to appear in the shops, one of the first items being irons, housewives in Kintbury plugged their irons into the light fittings, which were not 'earthed' so many a minor 'shock' occurred, though fortunately nothing serious – in Kintbury at least!

Housing in the village in early days was mostly rented and surprisingly this applied to many bigger properties such as Denford House and Elcot Park as well as humbler dwellings. Many Kintbury people owned blocks of property which they then let out at very low rents. This being so, they were mostly reluctant to keep their property in good repair. This was unfortunate for the tenants, many of whom had to endure wretched conditions. The most notorious houses were in Pig Lane (Laylands Green) and it was a relief when these were demolished round about 1936 and replaced with council houses. The building of many houses by the Hungerford Rural District Council in the 20s and 30s did much to improve living conditions for many families. This had to come to a temporary halt during the Second World War but resumed though rather slowly afterwards because of the lack of public money and materials. This meant that returning servicemen who had married during or soon after the war had terrible problems in getting 'housed', sometimes having to wait years for a house to be allocated. Some lived with parents in extremely overcrowded conditions and there was some 'squatting' in the by then unoccupied Army huts down at Barton Court and elsewhere. Gradually the situation improved and was helped as we come nearer to the present day as some families found a quicker and better way to house themselves was to buy their own home and this gradually became the norm for most people.

Then, another problem arose for Kintbury when the village was pressurised to allocate a considerable amount of land for new housing. The trouble was twofold, for in addition to being reluctant to see the village grow to the extent it has, nearly all the new houses were bought or allocated (if they were council properties) to new people wishing to come and live here. As elsewhere, house prices have increased so that many local people find it too expensive to buy within their native village. The last local authority housing to be built in Kintbury was at the Haven in 1974/75. Sheltered housing at Notrees was built in 1987. As we approach 2000 this problem is recognised by the Parish Council who have made strenuous efforts to find sites for 'affordable housing' specially for Kintbury residents but so far no landowner has been willing to release land for this purpose, or only with unacceptable strings attached.

Before 1935, or thereabouts, collection of household refuse was not undertaken by any public body in Kintbury. Until then householders disposed of their own refuse, usually by having a 'tip' somewhere within their own gardens and in later years, when these were dispersed, interesting fragments of pottery, old bottles, jars and other discarded items were turned up. Our own tip produced nothing more exciting than a chipped glass tankard, Victorian vintage, and an early 'Bovril' jar! There were other unofficial tipping places around the village which were used, one being somewhere near Sycamore Farm. When news came that the Rural District Council was to start collecting refuse in Kintbury the Parish Council had the job of dispersing these private tips and advertised for a contractor to get on with the task. When the proper R.D.C. collections started they were by horse and cart soon to be followed by custom-built refuse lorries. In those days the rubbish was taken to local pits at Irish Hill and at Haycroft on the other side of the A4. We end the century with our 'wheelie bins' and separate collections for paper, glass bottles and jars, tins and textiles, all these going for recycling.

In one hundred years we have come a long way. We may not be rich but we are certainly more affluent than most of our village forebears were in 1900 and our way of living has changed out of all recognition. Today we have much more leisure time and life has been made easier by the many labour saving devices which we have. Our choice of social activities, pastimes and entertainments is endless so that we can consider ourselves lucky to be living in this age. And yet, I wonder what Kintbury people who see in the year 2100 will make of us and our way of living today?

Women's Groups

For most of the century two women's movements have been very active in the village, particularly in the pre-Second World War years, when opportunities for women to take an interest in the world outside their immediate vicinity were, for most, very limited indeed. Notes for this chapter have been provided by Doreen Anstey (Mothers' Union) and Meg Tuckey (Women's Institute).

The Mothers' Union

The first organised women's group in the village was the Kintbury Branch of the Mothers' Union, which celebrated its 90th birthday in April 1999.

Mrs. Dunn invited the mothers of Kintbury to a meeting in the old laundry in the High Street in April 1909, at which they were addressed by Mrs. Wroughton of Woolley Park, Vice-President for Berkshire. Mrs. Woolley explained the MU's aim to promote Christian family life by prayer and practical support. The organisation's motto then was: 'Train up a child in the way he should go, and when he is old he will not depart from it.' Good sense surely that still holds today.

It was decided that Kintbury should form a branch, and Mrs. Catherine Edwards (wife of the Vicar) became the first Enrolling Member, an appointment she held with great success until the Edwards' retirement in 1928.

About 50 ladies attended the inaugural meeting and the Branch grew over these early years with 80 members from Kintbury attending a Deanery Festival in Newbury in 1922. It should be remembered that all women did not obtain an electoral vote until 1928, and the Mothers' Union was probably the first organisation which enabled women to come together and share the problems of their day.

Kintbury Branch has over the intervening years tried to fulfil the MU's aim by giving its members a programme which concerns the issues of the day, and also giving practical help to other local groups which need support. For instance, divorce was discussed way back in 1922; in 1944 Miss Duncan of Haworth House gave a talk on 'The Adolescent in the World Today' – a subject still current – and today has a prayerful as well as practical approach to helping drug offenders and the young homeless.

Branch numbers are nowadays much smaller than in the early years, reflecting the mobility and choices available to women today, but dedication to the Aims and Objectives of the movement are still the same.

Kintbury Women's Institute

Kintbury WI was founded in 1930 with the object of providing educational and leisure activities for the women of the village. As was usual at the time, the Institute was started by the local ladies; the inaugural meeting was chaired by Mrs. Clifton-Brown, wife of the MP and the first president was Mrs. Turner of Hungerford Park. The membership quickly rose to 140.

In the pre-war years the WI heard talks on travel in India, Switzerland, Japan and Fiji – think of the impact in those pre-television days. There were demonstrations of cookery and crafts, including one on 'The best use of an old mackintosh!' To go with the thrifty use of old mackintoshes, how about this recipe from a WI cookbook published in 1932:

SPARROW DUMPLINGS

Make a thick batter.

Put a lump of butter, rolled in

pepper and salt, in every sparrow,

mix them in the batter,

tie them in a cloth and boil for 1½ hours.

Serve with melted butter.

Any takers?

In March 1939, despite the threat of war, a group of intrepid members went on a trip to Belgium, led by the indefatigable Mrs. Baxter, a lady whose great organisational skills appear often in the reports of the Institute. By 1940 the reality of the war was affecting village life. The Coronation Hall was commandeered for troops and the meetings moved to the Wesleyan Hall.

The ladies of the WI rolled up their sleeves to help with the war effort. They formed a National Savings group; knitted hundreds of garments for the Forces, PoWs and the Merchant Navy; collected dried herbs and rosehips and most of all, they made jam! By permission of Lady Peterson, the stables at Inglewood Lodge were turned into a 'Jam Factory' and over the next few years WI members made over 2,000lb of jam as part of the Government's Fruit Preservation Scheme. The difficulties of living with food rationing are evident in a talk on overcoming the shortage of sugar and suet, and in the raffle of a lemon, which raised £1.

A Wartime recipe:

BREAKFAST CAKES
4oz self-raising flour
1 teaspoon egg powder
1 saltspoon salt
milk to mix to a stiff paste.
Drop spoonfuls into boiling fat.
Serve in place of eggs.

For some years after World War 2 Kintbury WI continued as before but the role of women in society was changing. In 1975 an Evening Institute was started to accommodate working wives and eventually the original afternoon WI decided to break away from the national WI organisation and do its own thing. This was very successful for some years, but recently the senior years have caught up with the members and the afternoon meetings have ceased. Meanwhile, the Kintbury evening WI group also decided to disband from the national organisation and with typical village enterprise, arrange their own programme. The group, now called the Kewi Club, is proving popular and enjoys a mixed programme with outside visits and talks ranging from 'The State of Israel' to 'Aromatherapy'. Should a national emergency arise in the future, there is no doubt that the talents of these women would be as useful as their predecessors proved.

*Early days in the
Women's Institute, c1930.*

From the Cradle to the Grave

by Sybil Flinn and Heather Turner

Health and Community Care

Finally, this book would be incomplete without an account of those we have depended on in childbirth, in illness and in our final moments – the doctors, nurses and healthcare support staff in Kintbury.

Kintbury has been fortunate in having doctors practising in the village not only throughout this century, but in the previous century as well, a record which other West Berkshire villages cannot claim, even today. From 1830 onwards the Doctors Lidderdale, father and son, looked after Kintbury. The Lidderdales lived at Osmington House in the High Street and were here until the early years of this century. The senior Lidderdale is commemorated by the stained glass window in the south wall of the nave of St. Mary's Church.

The lengthy Lidderdale practice was to be followed by that of Dr. Edmund Hemsted, who arrived as a young doctor in 1895 and was to remain in practice until his death 53 years later, another remarkable span of time and recorded on his tombstone in Christ Church cemetery. Dr. Hemsted's family came to England as émigrés from the Netherlands in the 16th century because of religious oppression, and his father, grandfather and great-grandfather were all doctors. Our Dr. Hemsted qualified before the age of 21 (possible then because the training period was shorter) and when he came to Kintbury aged 25, he built NoTrees, a large house in its own grounds approached by a drive from the High Street – site of the present sheltered housing and total care scheme which replaced the old house in 1987 and takes its name. His surgery was in the cottage at the entrance to his driveway, which has recently reverted to its original name of Threefold Cottage.

A direct link with Dr. Hemsted is Elsie Turfrey, who writes her story elsewhere in this book. Elsie's father came to Kintbury from Hungerford as Dr. Hemsted's chauffeur when the doctor acquired a motor car. Dr. Hemsted had previously done his rounds either on bicycle or pony and trap. Mr. Turfrey had 'converted' from being a coachman to driving a car, and his son eventually took over the chauffeur's position in turn. Being chauffeur to the doctor meant that you were on call as well, so Turfrey would be summoned to drive whenever Dr. Hemsted made a night call.

Notrees Kintbury.

Dr. Hemsted's home, demolished to build the present sheltered flats and care unit.

The Hemsted establishment with a full domestic staff was appropriate to a doctor's professional standing at that time. In the surgery, Mr. and Mrs. Powell lived on the premises, did the cleaning and took care of callers. Many still remember Miss Alberta Wake, who served for years as Dr. Hemsted's dispenser. In the earlier years of this century doctors used their own medicines – the time of the big drug companies had yet to come. In fact, even the humble aspirin had not been developed by Bayer, the German chemical company, until 1898. Miss Wake would also act as receptionist. Patients would usually receive their medication as they left the surgery, either dispensed from the doctor's stock remedies, or the dispenser would make up to the doctor's individual prescription.

Mrs. Hemsted was a very good tennis player, and all the family enjoyed this sport and there was, of course, a lawn tennis court in the grounds of NoTrees. Later, the Hemsted's great-grandson was to compete at Wimbledon, his name – Tim Henman.

There was a lot of grass to be cut at NoTrees and a large mowing machine pulled by a pony and a donkey wearing the approved leather hoof covers, so that their hoof marks would not spoil the grass. These animals were kept in the paddock at the back of the old vicarage.

Dr. Hemsted wanted to serve in the Royal Army Medical Corps in the First World War, but was turned down for health reasons, so that he continued in the Kintbury practice. However, during that war he had charge of several local hospital/convalescent homes, including Barton Court and Benham Park. He was also honorary surgeon to Newbury District Hospital, where he did much to improve facilities.

Later Dr. Norman Boulton came to join Dr. Hemsted's practice. He lived in Tuttles Cottage, and became very active in village affairs, serving as a member and later, Chairman of the Parish Council. Other members of the practice in 1939 were Dr. Lewis and Dr. Fletcher.

One essential member of the community in these earlier years was the midwife, as babies were rarely born anywhere else but in their parents' home. Kintbury had three midwives, who each spent many years in the village. Nurse Jordan was here during the 1920s and 30s and did her rounds on a 'sit up and beg' bicycle; Nurse Watson, who lived in one of the new council houses in Burtons Hill, and Nurse Anderson, who spent 22 years in Kintbury before retiring to her native Ireland.

In the years before the National Health Service was inaugurated in 1948 other doctors also practised in Kintbury. Best known of these was Dr. Jane Ferguson, who came in 1929 and had her home and surgery at the Mount House in Station Road. After 1945, Station Road also saw Dr. Hardy at the White House, and Drs. Irvine and Menzies at Kennet House for short periods.

Patent medicine advertisement of 1912.

During all the early years of the century healthcare had to be paid for – by fees to the doctor and payment for his medicine; payment to the midwife, and, should you die, payment too, to the woman who would come to lay you out! All this was to change with the coming of the National Health Service in 1948, which although planned much earlier had been delayed by the recessions of the 20s and 30s and then the Second World War.

The system of healthcare which we know in Kintbury today largely stems from the arrival of the third G.P., who was to make our wellbeing his lifetime's work. This was Dr. Noel Gillman, who was appointed in 1952 and lived at White Lodge in Newbury Street, making the small attached cottage into his surgery. The development of the NHS practice under Dr. Gillman can best be described in the words of Christine Anderson who came in those early years as District Nurse:

"In my earlier years (1957 approximately), there was only Dr. Noel Gillman and myself in the practice. I did combined duties – general nursing, Midwifery – all babies delivered at home; Health Visiting and Schools. Ante-natal, Post-natal and Immunisation Clinics were held in Dr. Gillman's surgery. Child Welfare clinics were held at the old Coronation Hall. Dr. Gillman worked alone: he only had a half day off weekly, and a weekend once a month. I had one day off weekly, so we were both tied to the area. The village was smaller then, the residents mostly local people. Eventually with the motorway etc., new people began moving in and changes took place. A School Nurse was appointed, relieving me of these duties. Dr. Gillman employed young trained doctors for a period of twelve months for experience, which was a great help to him, enabling him to have some definite time off duty.

"Midwifery cases now often went to hospital and when discharged were looked after by the midwife attached to Sandleford Maternity Hospital. This midwife also now attended Ante-natal clinics at Dr. Gillman's surgery, which now had three doctors. Health Visiting was transferred to a second Health Visitor at Hungerford. A new doctors' surgery was also built, so that all work was at the surgery with Nurse, Midwife, Health Visitor and Assistant Nurse all attached. Another surgery was also built at Woolton Hill and with its own doctor and staff worked in company with the Kintbury doctors. With Dr. Gillman as head of practice, all co-operated very well together for relief duties etc.

"All this was a gradual change, but in my estimation the patients were very well cared for and known personally to all the staff. I enjoyed every minute of my nursing career in Kintbury and surrounding areas, with very pleasant and appreciative patients."

How People Coped

Many people interviewed while compiling this book were asked the question 'How did you cope if you were ill before the National Health Service came in?' Surprisingly, it does not seem to be remembered as too great a problem, but then we are talking to the *survivors* – people by and large who have lived long and healthy lives. Obviously, it was not easy for some in the earlier years when many conditions now rarely encountered and now curable, were then fatal (diphtheria, tuberculosis, septicemia, for example). The parish magazines in the pre-1914 period record many deaths of infants and children alongside many parishioners who lived well past 'three score years and ten'.

In the pre-NHS days, doctors were usually only consulted for more serious conditions. Virtually no one would have contemplated going to the surgery for coughs, colds and such minor ailments. They relied on proprietary medicines increasingly available 'off the shelf' even in Kintbury stores, such as Chisletts. Advertising was not as tightly regulated as now, and adverts for the patent remedies promised wonder cures. Those of us who were children in the pre Second World War era, will remember being dosed with Scotts emulsion, Dr. Williams Pills for Pale People, Syrup of Figs and rubbed with camphorated oil for anything vaguely 'chesty'. Cough medicines were not so bad – Owbridges Lung Tonic had a great aniseed taste and could be addictive as its original formula contained laudanum!

So what happened when a doctor was needed, or hospital treatment prescribed? Under the 1911 Insurance Act, which came into force in 1913, insurance cover gave any worker earning less than £160 a year free treatment by a 'Panel' doctor – doctors could elect whether they would take 'panel' patients, rather as dentists with the NHS today. The agricultural worker's average wage at this time was about a pound a week. However, this scheme did not include wives or children. Neither did it pay for hospital nor dental treatment.

At about this time 'Hospital Schemes' had started up all over the country and did operate in Kintbury. Through these by paying 3d. per week, later increased to 6d., those participating were entitled to free hospital in-patient treatment. Also there were schemes operated by many doctors' practices whereby visits to the surgery were covered by a small weekly payment. However prescribed drugs, though there were less of them in early days, could become expensive and were not necessarily covered by the schemes described. In one case mentioned to us, drugs prescribed for one lady cost 26/- (£1.30) for a week's supply, and her husband earned £1.40. In that case the whole family rallied round and the problem was overcome. For those who had no

resources, the Poor Law was still in force and so they could seek help from the Overseer of the Poor but people were terrified of finding themselves in this situation and only in extreme cases would this help have been sought. One lady, recently widowed and with no income whatsoever did seek help but when she found that she was to be described on the form which had to be filled in as a 'pauper,' she declined help and fortunately found her own way out of her dilemma and into very respectable employment which resolved her problem. It is surprising that it was not until 1928 that the 'poor law' and its threat of the 'workhouse' came to an end, when it was replaced by 'National Assistance' and the 'Means Test', which was almost equally dreaded. However, local doctors did have regard for the needs of poorer patients. People did not go without treatment and it is likely that the fees which could be charged to richer people for the extra pampering which some demanded, helped to cover treatment of the less well off.

Home confinements were the norm, at which the District Nurse/Midwife would be in attendance. There were also homely, capable ladies, like Mrs. Wooldridge of Kintbury Farm cottages who could be called in to help a new mother for a few days after the birth; very necessary if there were other children in the family to be looked after, for women were not allowed to be up and about as soon as they are today and there was no such thing as husbands being allowed to take time off from work.

When the National Health Act came in, in 1948, the situation changed very rapidly. People soon got used to the luxury of visiting the surgery if they felt unwell or needed advice...and not having to pay! Demand grew. Medical research made more treatments possible, and the population of the village grew. We are extremely lucky to have our own Surgery and ancillary staff and drug dispensing service. Many villages in this area do not.

Our Community Services

We are lucky too to have a well-established Volunteer Service. We have our present Senior Practice G.P., Dr. Nick Yates to thank for helping to set this up in 1987 along with the then Vicar, Martin Gillham and local resident, Ken McDonald, with others. Then it was called the Kintbury Neighbourhood Scheme. It provided a Voluntary Driver Scheme through which those in need of transport were conveyed to hospital and to keep other medical appointments. This service is now much expanded and called the Kintbury Volunteer Group. Monthly lunches and Tea Dances are arranged, a Village Guide is periodically published, a part-time office operates from Thatchers Yard and the Group aims to respond to the needs of the village. Currently the Group is sponsoring and meeting the initial cost of the publication of this book.

Helpers raising money for the Old Folks Tea.

'Cradle to Grave' would not be complete perhaps without a mention of some groups which do not appear elsewhere in this book. The first is the 'Kintbury Kittens'. This is a Mother and Toddler group, which is a follow-on from previous similar gatherings. The current one meets at the Boys' Club and gives an opportunity for mums and children not old enough for play school to meet socially and exchange ideas and problems. Then we have the Kintbury Play Group which meets mornings in term time at the Coronation Hall. This is extremely well organised by the present Leader, Angela Hall and hopes one day to have its own premises. In days gone by such groups were never thought of as being necessary and it was probably the 'Wartime Nurseries' which were set up in the Second World War to allow mothers to participate in war work, which were the forerunners of today's groups for children under school age.

At the other end of the scale we have the groups for our Senior Citizens. Before the last war these were catered for by fairly regular 'Old Folks Teas'. These were run by enterprising ladies like Mrs. Childs and Mrs. Wooldridge who not only organised the teas with many other helpers, but also ran events beforehand to raise the money to pay for them. These included Jumble Sales, Carol Singing and many other events besides. And that was not all – for they also provided from among themselves the 'entertainment' for those do's.

After the last war, in 1959, Nancy Goulding, who lived at the Old Tannery in Station Road and Oswald Smith, who lived at Winding Wood, started what turned out to be an extremely successful club for the over 60s in Kintbury. This was called The Evergreens and it is still running today, though perhaps membership is somewhat less than in the very early days and the age-group higher. The club meets monthly and has a variety of activities, including outings, and Bingo is always popular. Altogether though it is a very different activity, run by itself, for itself, rather than the pre-war 'teas' which were organised by others and people sat at long tables in front of a 'set tea'.

Our newest group for our older residents is the 'Autumn Club.' This is quite a small gathering of those who are in the main less physically active, started by Ann Piper in 1981 and now run by Elizabeth Hopgood and her small committee. It is much appreciated for the warm and friendly atmosphere it creates and the special treats it provides from time to time.

So we come to the year 2000 with our voluntary and social activities in pretty good shape but our medical services sharing the strains being faced in this country generally and which we hope will be eased as we move into the next century.

Kintbury surgery yesterday (Dr. Gillman) ...
and today.

Our Changing Village

Overleaf you will find maps of the central village area dated 1900 and 1999 produced to identical scale. It is impossible within the confines of our page size to show the whole of Kintbury and still be readable. However, we hope these maps will give readers an impression of just how development has taken place over the century.

The area of the parish (8,671 acres) has not changed appreciably but the population which was 1,655 in 1900 is about 2,500 today, an increase of around 50%. Yet the number of houses has more than doubled, taking up farmland which surrounded the village in 1900.

Throughout the century Kintbury has remained a viable entity, but as this book has shown, there have been enormous changes. Few people now work in the village, but travel to jobs around the area and farther afield to London, Reading and other towns equally distant.

The Lawrence field, clearly shown in both maps as a central area of green space, is currently the subject of negotiation between our Parish Council and the Lawrence Trust, which it is hoped will safeguard its continued long term future as a green area for all to enjoy.

Kintbury has gained from the changes of the 20th century. It remains a vibrant community as the support for the activities of the various village groups demonstrates.

So now, as we go forward into the next millennium, what further changes will Kintbury see? We are already on the Internet (Web site www.kintbury.co.uk) and the rapid advances in computer technology and communication systems will inevitably mean that life will be different for all our residents. Let's hope that 'different' means 'better' and that the community spirit which has been so evident in the stories told in this book continues to thrive here during the next hundred years and well beyond.

The map on the right shows the boundaries of the Parish of Kintbury in 1999.
Overleaf are maps of the village centre in 1900 and 1999. The latter being reproduced by kind permission of Ordnance Survey ©Crown Copyright NC/99/020.
Both are to the scale shown below:

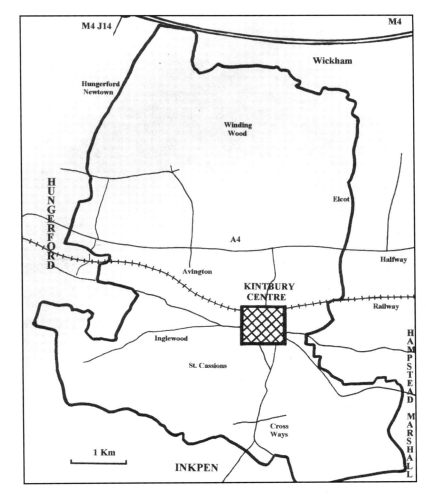

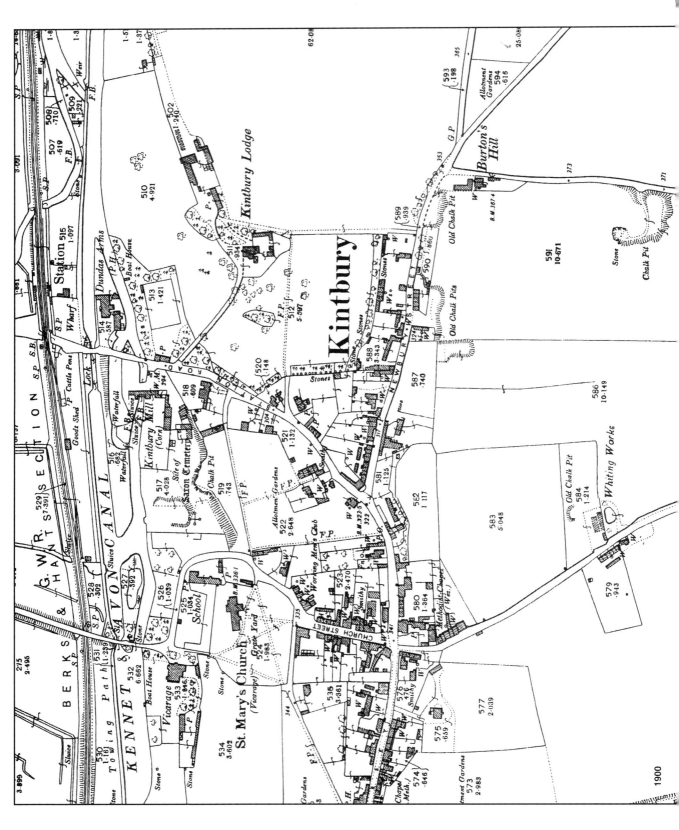

Kintbury

1999

Shops, Pubs and Interesting Houses

Our Shops

Some of the most significant changes which have occurred in Kintbury this century relate to our shops. Early on we know that there were at least twenty in the village, some having a dual role, like the sale of groceries and bread or drapery items. We had four grocers, three bakeries, three outfitters, one tailor, four blacksmiths, one wheelwright, two saddlers, a barber, stationer & newsagent, fishmonger, greengrocer and no less than five sweet shops. Today we have a butcher, baker, general stores, a potter and interior designers. We are lucky that as many as this have survived since many villages of our size have no shops at all, or maybe just one general store. It is interesting to take a step back in time and see where these early shops were –

IN STATION ROAD

Ernest Chapman's Outfitters, later Bob Sanders' Barbers and Sweet Shop (of late – Clover Antiques).

Killick's Stores – grocery and provisions (now Westmorland House).

Sweet Shop run by Mr. Beavis the Carrier (now 7, Station Road).

Shelldrakes, Saddlers (now Planit Interiors).

James Abrahams' first grocery and bakery (now York House and Barn Cottage).

Arthur Lawrence's Corn Sales and Coral Order Office (now part of The Old Barn).

North's Saddlers, then Butchers, then Cycle & Hardware Shop (now Tweazles).

Tailor's Shop (now Pound Cottage).

White's Blacksmith's Forge (now Forge Cottage).

Sawyer's Drapery and Sweet Shop (now The White House).

IN NEWBURY STREET

Shaw's Dairy and Sweet Shop (now Wayside Cottage).

George Giles, Carrier – groceries and paraffin (of late our Filling Station).

IN HIGH STREET

Page and Lockyer, Newsagent and Stationer (now two cottages).

Blacksmith's Forge (just after No. 6 High Street).

Rolfe's Bread and Cake Shop (now No. 7).

Willoughby's Fishmongers and Greengrocery (now Kintbury Pottery).

John and Richard Swales, Pot and Pan Makers & Repairers (now No. 32)

Butcher's Shop run by Mr. Budd and later Dennis Hunt (now No. 48).

IN CHURCH STREET

Chislett's Stores – Grocery, Bakery and Drapery (now Corner Stores).

Butcher's Shop, various owners including Pete Thatcher (still a Butchers).

Wheelwright's Shop, then a garage (now part of the The Square housing development).

Ernest Chapman, Outfitter (his second shop – now Kintbury Bakery).

Blacksmith's Forge (now 'Greystones' after rebuilding).

James Abrahams' second shop after moving from Station Road – Grocery and Bakery (now Church House).

Ernest Chapman's first shop in Station Road, between the Wars.

IN INKPEN ROAD

Behind The Barley Mow Public House – a small shop selling sweets and tobacco (after closure as a pub, The Barley Mow became a Butcher's Shop run by Dennis Hunt who moved from High Street. It is now a private house).

Miss Bance's Sweet & General Shop – a tiny shop in her cottage, now demolished, location next to track called The Cowlease.

Our Pubs

There were eight in the early 1900s. Those remaining are the Blue Ball, Dundas Arms and The Prince of Wales. Those which have closed are The Axe and Compass (private house now), The Nag's Head (private house), The Olive Branch, junction of Post Office and Folly Roads, Inkpen, but actually in Kintbury Parish, (now demolished and replaced by two houses), The Plasterers' Arms (now The Old Plasterers) and the The Three Horse Shoes (private house).

Our remaining pubs have changed hardly at all in outward appearance in 100 years. Refurbished internally, each has retained its own particular character and its own 'regulars'. In case we should think that we must be rather short of 'watering holes' now as compared with earlier days we should add that now we have five other licensed premises – the Elcot Park Hotel, the Inglewood Health Hydro, the Bistro Roque plus the Kintbury Rangers Football Club and the Kintbury Bowls Club, as well as an Off-Licence at the Corner Stores.

OTHER BUILDINGS OF INTEREST

Some of these have been mentioned in previous chapters but are listed here with others which space and time have prevented us mentioning in this book but which perhaps may be the subject of further study at some time –

The Old Laundry (demolished).

Hungerford Park (18th century mansion, demolished).

Templeton House (demolished).

The Round House (toll house on London to Bath Road at the Halfway, demolished).

Barton Court.

Barton Grove (a 'twin' of the Old Vicarage).

Forbury House.

Denford House (Norlands Training college).

Elcot Park (18th century attractive house now part of hotel).

Wallingtons (now St. Cassian's).

Inglewood House (now The Hydro).

Avington Manor.

Additionally we have a number of very interesting and often attractive farmhouses, almost all built by the two large estates – Craven and Sutton who once owned much of the land within Kintbury Parish. These houses, now mostly privately owned, include Kintbury Holt, Watermans, Clapton, Radley and Wawcott.

Blacksmith's and Wheelwright's shop in Church Street, early 1920s.

Acknowledgements

We are most grateful to the authors who have contributed articles to this book, and to those listed below for their help with memories, photographs, drawings and other material.

Enid Anisewski • John Allen • Christine Anderson • Colin Bailey • Margaret Bailey • Nick Bailey
Richard Bankes • James Barnett • Lil Bentley • 'Sis' Braidwood • Penny Brookman • Derek Clements • Mabel Cook
Kath Culley • Hilda Dance • Charles Dance • John Dellow • Ethel Druce • Peter Durrant • Marjorie Fraser
Keith Gilbert • Anstace Gladstone • Doris Greenough • Joyce Greenough • Mollie Griffiths • Christine Hall • Ted Hall
Ray Hamblin • Ted Hill • John Hull • Sonia Johnson • 'Bubbles' Knight • Peter Lambourn • Eileen McCullum
Patricia Mead • Clare Minchin • Henry Moore • Bernard Morris • David Morris • Thora Morrish
Lilian Newman • William Newton • Ivan Osborne • Kit Palmer • Don Panting • Queenie Panting • Keith Plank
Tony Preston • Barbara Radbourne • Nora Rose • Joan Sadler • Geoffrey Sampson • Richard Sampson
Valerie Shirley • George Smith • Angela Stansfeld • Lilian Taylor • St. Cassians Centre • Eileen Thatcher
Denis Turner • Patrick Turner • Joyce Warne • Nancy Wild • Judy Wilson.

. . . to the following for photographs copied from their collections:

Sue Hopson • Stan Thomas • The Collier Collection • Peter Bloodworth • Brian Frost • AWE Aldermaston.

. . . to these organisations for material made available from their records:

The West Berks Heritage Service • Newbury Library • Newbury Weekly News • Berkshire County Archive
Hungerford Historical Association • Kintbury St. Mary's School • Kintbury Parish Council
Kennet & Avon Canal Trust • De la Salle Community • Trencherwood plc • Rural History Centre, Reading.

Kintbury Volunteer Group,
Thatcher's Yard, Church Street,
Kintbury, West Berkshire RG17 9TR.